"*Coming Home* is a whip-smart combination of being and doing. I heartily recommend his wise and vulnerable contribution to a vitally needed conversation on true connection."

—Dave Workman
author, leadership coach, and president of Elemental Churches

"*Coming Home* is an engaging and enjoyable read on the reasons we need community. Jon offers very practical insights on living into biblical community and why all Christians so desperately need it. Jon's humor allows some awkward fears and concerns about community to be addressed in not only biblical, but tangible ways. . . . If you want to seriously embrace the call of community, read through this book with other people who have a vision for what is possible."

—Bubba Justice
National Coordinator of Vineyard USA

"God created every human heart with a longing for true community. This book is a valuable guide towards finding the type of Christian community that we so desperately need. Jon brings brilliant insights into common everyday life, and he knows what he's talking about because he lives it with authenticity."

—Joel Gorveatte
Lead Pastor, Moncton Wesleyan Church (Canada)

"Jon's easy conversational style and his clever structure make *Coming Home* a delightful read. The topic of Christian community is vital in an era of increasing virtual living wherein the Scriptural directive to 'assemble together' is being reinterpreted and lost. His is essential guidance, especially for Christian leaders, and also for those desiring a closer walk with Christ."

—Phil Bishop
Professor Emeritus, University of Alabama

"In his book *Coming Home*, Jon does a brilliant job of giving language to this elusive word called *community*. Deep down we all desire it, we were even created for it, but few of us ever find it. Jon leads us on a personal journey of discovery as he attempts to find true community. His conversational style, blended with just the right amount of humor, will keep your mind and heart longing for more If you're looking to get more out of life and relationships, this is a must-read."

—Kevin Fischer
Lead Pastor, Miami Vineyard Community Church

"As you read what Jon has to say it will become clear to you that Jon speaks from both his head and his heart and his words will both encourage you and motivate you to live out your Christian faith in community with renewed hope."

—Jonathan Cook
Marriage and Family Therapist

"In *Coming Home* Jon challenges the idea that ministry or leadership have to be lonely, and he offers a vision of real community that is inspiring for church leaders and lay people alike."

—Adam Russell
Lead Pastor, Campbellsville Vineyard Church

"If you've been part of a church for any amount of time, you've heard a thousand times that you need community. This book helped me to understand why I need community, what community really looks like, and why I should persevere in community even when it is hard."

—Ben Talmadge
Lead Pastor, Grace Church

"Jon Quitt is a reliable voice in the realm of gospel community, not only because he is well versed in what Scripture teaches in regard to it, but because he embodies community through and through."

—Shaun Faulkner
Lead Pastor, Soma Church

Coming Home

Coming Home

Discovering, Cultivating, and Enjoying the Best Community of Your Life

JON QUITT

WIPF & STOCK · Eugene, Oregon

COMING HOME
Discovering, Cultivating, and Enjoying the Best Community of Your Life

Copyright © 2019 Jon Quitt. All rights reserved. Except for brief quotations in critical publications or reviews, no part of this book may be reproduced in any manner without prior written permission from the publisher. Write: Permissions, Wipf and Stock Publishers, 199 W. 8th Ave., Suite 3, Eugene, OR 97401.

Wipf & Stock
An Imprint of Wipf and Stock Publishers
199 W. 8th Ave., Suite 3
Eugene, OR 97401

www.wipfandstock.com

PAPERBACK ISBN: 978-1-5326-9109-6
HARDCOVER ISBN: 978-1-5326-9110-2
EBOOK ISBN: 978-1-5326-9111-9

Manufactured in the U.S.A.   09/04/19

To Amy and the years of ploughing hard ground alongside of me. Also, to the group of men and women who grace our home each week—you deserve much of the credit because you have been the guinea pigs in our search for life-giving friendship.

Contents

Introduction | xi
1. Building the House | 1
2. The Foyer is for Introductions | 15
3. The Kitchen is for Cultivating | 34
4. The Dining Room is for Depth | 56
5. The Living Room is for Longevity | 78
6. The Garage is for Growing Up | 92
7. The Bedroom is for Covenant | 107
8. Questions and Answers | 122

Bibliography | 137

Introduction

THE CHURCH WORLD IS changing. Church people are changing. If you've stepped into the local mega Christian complex in recent years the predominant message seems to be *Go Big*! Enormous stages filled with pretty people. Larger-than-life pastors giving us self-help soundbites that seem to be more self than help. We often walk out of the crowded auditoriums wondering if what we just experienced is all there is. Surely there is more to the Christian life—a God-filled life—than the one-hour drive through.

I'm not knocking the Sunday morning gathered church. I'm a pastor, in fact. I enjoy seeing friends on a regular Sunday schedule. I love standing and singing. I look forward to sitting with a bible open, being challenged by the Good News of Jesus and his Kingdom reign over my life. I encourage anyone—everyone—to connect to a local church congregation. The gathered church is an imperfect, but beautiful expression of where we begin in our journey with God and others.

However, simply going to church is not enough. Sundays are not the goal. Even the language of going to church implies an activity we do. Church becomes a box to check, not a people to walk with. Church gets relegated to the category of going to the gym or balancing our check book. We do it because it is good for us. Not necessarily because we have found a deep well of life.

Weekly I hear stories from those I sit with of their disappointment with the corporate entity called the church. They wonder why it feels shallow, anemic. Many have felt abandoned, heartbroken, disillusioned with the gathered church. I don't defend the church. It's no use. She is a mess. Instead, I do my best to redirect my friend's attentions. I help them realign their expectations.

When Jesus invited his disciples to leave their boats and nets he wasn't inviting them into a global organization, but a family. His formation of the

Introduction

church was firstly grounded in his sacrifice for us and secondly, our sacrifice and commitment to one another. The desire that we all have to live and walk with others in deep, meaningful ways is a kind of "eternity set in our hearts" (Ecclesiastes 3:11) that God placed there from the beginning. As we find, cultivate and enjoy this community we discover we have unearthed this little treasure that God buried long before we knew it was there.

To get the most out of this book, I would encourage you to read it with others. This isn't a ploy to get you to buy multiple copies of the book, but an invitation to begin to do something meaningful with someone else. Read the book and discuss it. Apply it. Take some chances.

In doing so, you might find yourself in the coming weeks and months coming home to a different house. Not necessarily a different address, but a house that is now teeming with life and people who know you and love you and are committed to a life that matters.

1

Building the House

A SHIFT IN CULTURE does not come all at once. There is rarely an avalanche of new sounds, thoughts, and ideas that crashes in and changes everything. Change happens one trickle at a time. Change usually begins in the arts, then in music, then in philosophy, and finally, in theology. Christians, it turns out, are usually the last to find out what the world is thinking. And by that time, change is happening again. Jesus' followers are often a generation behind on what is happening around us. However, this is not true about all things. One place of philosophical and spiritual geography where the church planted its flag long before anyone else even knew it existed was the place and practice of community.

Community has a definition. I'll get to the technicalities in a minute, but it's more important to recognize that community has connotations. And it's our connotations, our understanding of words, which determine how we live. For example, my family lives in a city. This is our community. We love our city. Our community has two universities, a community college, 84 restaurants, and 240 churches, along with one mayor and 12 city council members who govern this community well. I shop, worship, and walk my dog alongside these community members. But this is not the community I mean when I think about the kind of community my soul aches for.

I also live in a neighborhood community. We share streets, water lines, and a common identity of suburban dwellers. We cook out together, swim in each others' pools, and watch each others' kids when needed. These are good people whom I live alongside. We know our neighbors' names and are quite fond of a few. We have community in our neighborhood—but it's still not quite what we all long for.

I also belong to a church. Not a large church, but not a small church either. Every week several hundred gather. We sit in rows, sing our own particular liturgy, let God's Word work on us, and then we leave. We shake some hands, hug some necks, and catch up on the latest broken arm, lost job, and annoying boss. Someone systematically turns off the lights and that is our cue to leave the building. Some leave together. A meal will seal our time. Others, most others, leave as they came . . . alone. We get in our cars still wondering if this is what community, real community, is supposed to look like. We think to ourselves, "We shared time, we shared scriptures, and we even had a moment when prayer happened over us. Surely this is community!" And it is. But it's still not the kind of community I'm talking about—not the kind of community we long for while we drive home from church by ourselves.

One thing we all share in common is a desire to be known deeply by people. Somewhere in the recesses of our hearts, we want something from other people that is hard to describe. It's like a dream that fades too quickly. Or a disjointed memory that may be our own, but we just can't be sure. We long for it, but we aren't really able to describe what the "it" is. Our hearts remind us that the storms of life are coming. The waves are building. We do not want to be in this storm by ourselves.

But what do we do?

One of the first acts of God on behalf of his newly created Adam was an act of community. "It is not good for you to be alone" (Genesis 2:18). And what proceeded was the gift, from the hand of God, of another person. Eve, in fact, came from Adam. She was literally part of him. And that is where community begins. We recognize we are part of each other. No getting around the scar. Your wound is my wound. A fence or cubicle may separate us, but when we embrace the gift and calling of community, we are able to touch the scar of our own missing rib and embrace the one who holds it in his hand. Community is painful and beautiful. We can see it from a distance—we catch a glimpse of it in others, yet it continues to elude us. So we set aside the dream of real community, settling for the fictional community found on a screen. What our hearts long for has been replaced by a quick comment on social media, an emoji smiley face, and a promise to get lunch soon. Hours are spent attempting to develop this fictional community. But when the screen goes black, so go our hearts.

My wife Amy and I work in a church. That's my job. I love it. Twenty years ago, we decided to spend our life serving people inside and outside the church. We were told it would feel a bit like living in a fishbowl. We were told to watch our step and tread carefully because people are always watching. I was already feeling some of this, but then it was reinforced by a hundred different conversations with other pastors and ministry folk. "You know you can't have any real friends in ministry. It's lonely in leadership. Get used to it." My wife and I just accepted these statements as gospel truth because, after all, these were seasoned pastors and missionaries who had walked with Jesus since I was still wetting my bed. But over time, something in our hearts, and more importantly, what we read in the Scriptures, told us that what these men and women believed was wrong. It is possible to live in deep, gospel-centered, burden carrying, open heart, life-transforming community. We asked around to some other pastors and their families who were not totally convinced that ministry has to mean friendlessness, and they told us, "Deep friendship is possible, but not probable." Not the answer we were looking for. But we had hope. More importantly, we had faith that what God provided for Adam, and what he provided for countless others in the church, He would provide for us and for those we sought to do life with.

Amy was the first to communicate this need she had to walk deeply with a few other people. Honestly, I didn't get it in the beginning. We were already so busy with bible studies, outreach events, and church services that I usually went to bed exhausted, and frankly, fulfilled. I thought, "Do we really need one more thing?" Some of this, I now realize, is because I'm a man. Most men find fulfillment in what they do. In contrast, most women find fulfillment in who they're doing it with. Thankfully, gender is not the trump card in what is true or right—the scripture is always our standard for what is true. It has been interesting to see how my wife's tenderness leans into relationship with people long before my heart does. But because of this disconnect between our desires for gospel community, it took us a few years to know where spiritual north was.

Not long after we started our church, we began to pray that God would bring a family into our lives that we could connect with. We didn't have any language at the time for what we really needed or longed for. We just knew it would be good for our family and for our souls to begin to walk deeply with others.

We made a list. I'm not joking. We made a list. Our list didn't quite read like a seventh grade girl's dream boy list, but it was close. We started with the stuff that was obvious. They needed to be married. It would be great if they had kids. Jesus lovers? Yep. Then we began to narrow the scope. Ideally, the age of the kids needed to be close to our kids' ages. Their home needed to be close by. Theological connection was also important. But we figured we'd ask them about their position on the doctrine of penal substitutionary atonement after we were best friends. We eventually finished the list and then got to work searching for the perfect family.

The beauty of starting our own church is that we had a steady flow of young couples visiting our building every Sunday. Of course, we knew these were not just prospects for our budding church—they were all being quietly interviewed to be our bosom buddies for life. We'd go out to dinner with one couple and I would be convinced these two had been sent from God. I was already dreaming about going on family vacations with these people, then we would get in the car and Amy would say, "That was a nightmare! She's crazy!" The next weekend it would be the exact same scenario, but this time I was the one crying foul. I can remember more than one dinner in which I had to give my wife the "secret signal" under the table, letting her know that it was time for us to run!

The first few years in the life of our young church were fraught with relational disappointments for us. Many men and women in our new faith family seemed to be connecting in deep ways. It was beautiful to see. But Amy and I were finding it difficult to find others we could do life with. There seemed to be a secret room where all of the perfect friendships were born. The problem was that that no one was telling us where it was.

Then we met Joe and Patty. Joe and Patty were attending another church at the time and a mutual friend of ours set us up on a date of sorts. It sounds weird, but that's exactly what it was. This friend said, "I think you guys would hit it off. Meet here at this time and I'll get them there too!" Out of desperation we showed up, and against all odds, a friendship began. That first night was easy and filled with chemistry. The conversation flowed as if we had been friends for years. We laughed hard, and even shared some tender places in our lives that were reserved for those who knew us best. After finishing dinner and a bottle of wine, we knew it was time to get the kids in the bed. On the way home, neither Amy nor I knew what to say. It felt too good to be true. Had we found the unicorn? Had we stumbled upon the beginning of our ever-elusive community?

BUILDING THE HOUSE

Before we move on, let's make sure we're on the same page with our words. Words matter. Language matters. I'm not talking grammar or syntax, though that matters as well. When words like community are thrown around, it's because we assume everyone has the same working definition. But that's not always true. So words, our mutual understanding of what we mean, matter. Just ask any three people from multiple generations what a particular word means. The word gay, for example, in the 1950s was a description of someone who was happy. But now gay means something entirely different.

So definitions matter. In a moment, I'm going to give you my working definition for community. You may have a different definition, but for the sake of our conversation, a unified vocabulary is paramount. This definition has evolved as my understanding of scripture has grown, and as my experience of Jesus-centered relationships has taken shape. I agree with every word of the definition (I mean, I did write it). However, for full disclosure, I have yet to experience all of it firsthand. Part of this faith journey of community is knowing there are some things that are true even if I haven't yet seen them in person. Some of what I write feels like a third-hand myth that was whispered to me by a gypsy. In the same way that Moses saw the Promised Land, but never set foot in it, community is sometimes beyond the mountains.

Before I give you my definition for community, consider a few other common definitions[1]:

1. A social group of any size whose members reside in a specific locality, share government, and often have a common cultural and historical heritage.

2. A locality inhabited by such a group.

3. A social, religious, occupational, or other group sharing common characteristics or interests, and perceived or perceiving itself as distinct in some respect from the larger society within which it exists (usually preceded by the—e.g., the business community; the community of scholars).

4. A group of associated nations sharing common interests or a common heritage.

1. Dictionary.com, "community," accessed May 20, 2019, https://www.dictionary.com/browse/community

5

These definitions don't really do justice to the word community, do they? It's like they just defined vanilla ice cream by saying that it's a combination of milk, sugar, cream, nonfat milk solids, corn syrup solids, mono- and diglycerides, guar gum, dextrose, sodium citrate, artificial vanilla flavor, sodium phosphate, carrageenan, disodium phosphate, cellulose gum, and vitamin A palmitate. Do these combined ingredients create ice cream? Technically they do. I looked it up. But when was the last time you had a hankering for non-fat milk solids? We all know that ice cream is so much more. My mind drifts to a hot summer day a few years ago with my 10-year-old daughter on my arm. We're walking into the local ice cream shop for a date. We know that ice cream brings with it an expectation of nostalgia, silly laughter, and drips down the chin. When my daughter wants ice cream with her dad, she's asking for more than a double scoop of diglycerides. She is asking for a memory.

In the same way, community is more than meetings, dinner dates, and church fellowships. Those may be ingredients in the mixing bowl of community. The parts, however, do not equal the whole. Not only is community more than those elements, it requires more from us. Finding it, or more likely, developing it, can be like cooking without a recipe. I don't mean you are simply making things up for your meat loaf. I just mean that you know what it's supposed to taste like, so it takes some time to get it just right. You grab a little oregano. You cut up some thyme. Still not right? A splash of ketchup. Then a little more panko. Sometimes you get it right and sometimes you toss it and go for take-out. Cooking that way is so much harder, but the best cooks I know cook like that.

Those that develop the kind of community we're going to talk about start with a clear gospel recipe, and then sprinkle in what is needed to make it palatable and tasty in their context. Community—graceful, thoughtful, patient, and missional community—takes time and intention.

THE DEFINITION

With my wife, I have helped cultivate a small group of friendships—a band of community—for many of the sixteen years since our church began. Twelve to fifteen people meet in our home every week to eat, pray, cry, make sushi, and spur each other on to love Jesus and each other like never before. I love these people. But every time a new semester begins, knowing we will have a few different people join us, I give a speech and tell them, "This is not community." I get a cock-eyed look from the newcomers because that is exactly what they thought they were coming for. I say it again. "This is not community. This is the beginning of community—this is the opportunity for community to develop." And then I give them this definition.

Community is where we are joyfully submitted to a diverse group of men and women who love one another in spite of our frailties and enough to call each other to deep repentance so that we might walk deeply together through the seasons of life in a way that keeps Jesus at the center of our relationships.

Let's spend a minute unpacking this.

Joyfully submitted . . .

No one likes begrudging love. Joyful submission to one another means we lay down our rights and preferences because we understand that when we serve others, we are serving Christ—and then we get the joy for it. Submission only works when it is done with a tender heart that is inclined towards God. Joy comes as we submit our hearts to God because we believe he is out for our best. In the same way, joy is multiplied in relationships as we all submit to one another.

. . . to a diverse group of men and women

Homogeny happens without the grace and power of God. Homogeny means like one another. The thing is, we naturally gather with those like us. Moms with moms. Dads with dads. College kids with college kids. Like-mindedness and chemistry are fine, and they are welcomed, but they can never be the metric that defines who gets to stay. Entire communities have been developed around getting people together who are just like each other. However, the problem with homogeny is that we're rarely challenged to grow if we fail to embrace diversity.

. . . who love one another in spite of our frailties and enough to call each other to deep repentance

Love is not contingent on perfection. Thank God for that. In fact, scripture reminds us that ". . .while we were still sinners, Christ died for us" (Romans 5:8).

That is, the most dramatic expression of love was given in the light of the greatest rebellion. And because of that truth, deep and robust community is only developed when the sin-stained hearts of people are dragged under the bright light of gospel friendship. Walking deeply demands that we look past each frailty and into what is possible by the grace of God.

. . . so that we might walk deeply together through the seasons of life

Walking deeply is the key. Nobody really needs another water cooler conversation about the Kardashians. Our lives are made for people in each new season of birth, rebirth, and even death. The newborns and the empty nesters both need a deep bond that bridges the years of change. Those who are facing cancer, divorce, and rehab all need a people who are willing to go the distance for their sakes. Depth comes with time, but it also comes through active participation in the bright and dismal seasons of life.

. . . in a way that keeps Jesus at the center of our relationships.

Scratching the itch of loneliness is not the point. Even the pursuit of deep relationships misses the mark. Jesus must be the treasure of our relationships because people can't be the goal. Jesus must be the goal and the treasure of every one of our relationships. He alone satisfies. Walking deeply with men and women through long seasons gives them access to our broken places, which enables them to offer the help we need to re-align our hearts back to God. Filling our homes with the laughter of friends and our nights and weekends with endless dinners and engagements may feel like the prize, but none of that is what our souls need. Extinguishing the fires of isolation isn't enough.

Jesus is the point of life together.

I like technical definitions like the one I just gave you, but if I had to boil this idea down to one word, it would be the word family. Life together and long-term.

Old and young learning and growing. Dense and delightful seasons. Growing up and sending out. Meals shared and tears shed.

All of this describes a family. But I don't want to make any assumptions about your understanding of the word family. For many, if not most, family has the scent of perennial absenteeism rather than granite-like security. But once again, for our conversation, we all have an innate hope of what a family could or should be. That's what we're after. People—diverse people, all kinds of people—around a table and doing life the way it was meant to be lived . . . together.

RIGGED TO FAIL

Some messages are birthed in our hearts by God. He drops them in like a care package or a kind gift on our birthday. Other messages are burned in our hearts by experience and pain. This thing of community, this message that we all know is intuitively sacred, has been a little bit of both for me—God breathed and also sin-stained. Joy-filled and heart-bruised. Sacred and scary. In every season Amy and I are increasingly hesitant to invite others into our home. We feel both the sting of loneliness and the pull of God, and yet we are still buffeted by the fear of getting hurt. I think, I'm barely healed up from the last go round, and yet I want to stay in the fight.

Pastorally, I'm afraid for those we're inviting in. I have a keen awareness of this experiment. It may not work. We're not splitting the atom, but dangerous things are at play when we seek this thing out. We are selling something that is true and good and infinitely satisfying, but something that is also infinitely hard and uncomfortable.

Most don't make it. The promise of life-together is sometimes never realized. Some throw up their hands, confessing they never really believed in the fairy tale to begin with. I am not angry with them. I'm not angry with God either. He knows what he is doing. I am often disappointed with myself, though, for my impatience. People are finicky, I think. In part, I am expecting more from community, more from people, than God actually promises. Bosom buddies and vacation pals aren't really what God describes in the pages of scripture. Burden bearers (Galatians 6:2) and heart wounders (Proverbs 27:6) are more in line with God's picture of community. Communal living and cloistered families sound romantic, but that's just not the reality of the kingdom. When God calls us to live together (Acts 2:44–46) . . . in unity (1 Corinthians 1:10) . . . as companions (Philippians 4:3) . . . on mission, it really is a call to die.

There are so many reasons that a person shouldn't get into community, dozens of legitimate grievances, in fact, that the heart is rigged to fail. I'm not throwing rocks here. We all live in glass houses. But when I begin to have a conversation with others about what is possible or hopeful or supernaturally tenable, I see hearts begin to rise and then give way to a hundred reasons why it won't work.

"I've been hurt by the church."

I know. Me too. We church people are such dopes. Idealistic and naïve with all those bumper sticker slogans and bad sermon titles. Big buildings and slick programs. Lots of promises and not a lot of delivering. But here's the thing, you went, you listened, you even dropped anchor there for a season. And the most surprising thing happened—things began to make sense. The fog was lifting and for the first time in years, you saw how God was knitting you together in a family.

And then the other shoe dropped. The pastor didn't show up before your surgery. Or your Sunday School teacher offended you. The church hospitality coordinator ironically snubbed you. The friends you made weren't being friends. It happens in a million different ways. In the critical moments when we really needed someone to shepherd our hearts, we got hurt. Damaged. Offended. Left alone. Let down. Probably all of the above.

So you made a decision in your anger. "I knew it. I knew this was too good to be true. I'm outta here. You really can't trust anyone!" You left. Or maybe you feel they left you. But either way, the community you had hoped for seemed more impossible than ever.

"I can do life on my own."

Giving up on abiding and long-term community doesn't happen all at once. It's usually a result of one disappointing friendship after another. And we think to ourselves, "I've tried to go deep with these people 87 times. I'm done! Apparently, what I want and what my heart longs for is just an anomaly." That's when we give up and determine in our hearts that we can do life all by ourselves.

I can't tell you how many times Amy and I have sat in our living room on a Friday night, alone, disappointed, and jealous. We'll scroll down the social media walls of our hundreds of "friends" as they are advertising how great a time they are having with everyone but us. We have fumed, cried, argued. But mostly we have parroted the words, "I guess we're on our own. It's just you and me, babe."

"I'm not into group therapy."

We've all had those friends—eternally wounded and undeniably broken. Soul suckers is what I call them when no one is listening. Every time you get within ten feet of them, they emotionally throw up on you. They are compelled to give you the 25-minute tragic narrative of their lives and explain why everyone around them is to blame. When you're finally able to peel yourself away from them, you feel like you need to take a shower. You know that person?

Nobody wants to be in the kind of community where all we end up doing is licking each other's wounds—perpetual pity parties. We pass on what is possible because we're fairly confident that the word community is code for a weekly counseling session.

"I don't want people up in my business."

Who does? We think our frailties, addictions, woundings, unforgiveness, and poor decisions are ours alone to deal with. So when we say no to community, it's a no-brainer. Letting people into the inner workings of our lives means they will see the real us, and that is dangerous. It's enough work keeping up our current image without the added drama that comes with people actually knowing our junk.

So we pass on what could be. We settle for surface relationships. Facebook, Twitter, Instagram, or whatever tool is available to feign authenticity while keeping a comfortable distance from real relationships. Or we medicate ourselves with food, alcohol, and work. We convince ourselves that keeping our head down is how we get through this thing. Worst of all, we begin to believe that what's true of our screen-based community is true of real community—that it doesn't really require honesty.

Who's got the time?

Twenty-five million people report they work a minimum of 49 hours a week. Another eleven million report that they work 59 hours a week.[2] We are a worn-out generation. Single moms, stay-at-home dads, the upwardly

---

2. Jena McGregor, "The Average Workweek is Now 47 Hours," Last modified September 2, 2014, Accessed June 6, 2018, https://www.washingtonpost.com/news/on-leadership/wp/2014/09/02/the-average-work-week-is-now-47-hours

mobile, or the minimalist by choice—we all face these challenges. We are all navigating little league practice, soccer games, graduate school, or last-minute office deadlines. All are understandable reasons that community is an impossibility.

Time, of course, is the real currency of our culture. And most of us are time poor. If we could trade in dollars and cents for a moment of silence or a cup of coffee with a friend, we would. But we don't know how to stop the merry-go-round. We're stuck—stuck in a race in which no one wins.

It's not that we don't want community, but how in the world do we fit it into our schedule? Who has the time and emotional bandwidth? How do we prioritize between what is important and what is essential? We think to ourselves, "If I can only do a couple of things in my 168-hour week, cultivating bonds with those outside my gene pool isn't going to make the cut."

Time continues to be the cruelest taskmaster, cracking its whip at us and putting to death any hope of a real life with people. The hands of the clock spin faster and faster and before we can blink, years have passed without bringing us any closer to what we know is possible. And worse yet, we sink into despair and self-condemnation. We know the extra time binge watching Netflix on Saturday wasn't the right investment when we find that what we needed was someone to cry with us, laugh with us, or talk us off the ledge on Sunday. We all know community matters, but its importance gets relegated to our tomorrows.

PROXIMITY AND PROVIDENCE

Often, when people are asked, "When was the last time you experienced true community?" it's not uncommon to hear them share a story about college roommates and the natural way their lives were woven together. Late night dinners and 2 a.m. pizza runs. Even more, these strangers became built-in comforters when the romance imploded. Cheerleaders when finals were kicking their butts. Counselors and burden-bearers and best friends were who they became in spite of the fact that we had no real hand in choosing who they were. More than likely, an anonymous person in campus housing cast the die. It's natural for us to look back on those magical times and wonder, why was it so easy? And more importantly, why is it so hard now that I'm all grown up?

What we end up discovering, as adults with responsibilities and families and mortgages to pay, is that we don't just stumble into the kind of community we're talking about.

For many of us, the community we formed in college was beautiful and real. I have no intention of demeaning it like some kind of middle school romance. It had depth and spontaneity. But what we had back then was proximity and providence.

We're all grown up now and we don't live in a crowded dorm. The proximity of people has disappeared. We don't walk to class anymore and see friendly faces on the quad. We're now commuting long distances and sitting with strangers. After a day's labor we close the garage door behind us. And even though we have neighbors near us (proximity), it feels different. It is different.

Providence was on our side too. Not that God isn't in control now. He is. But our college experience was a very real surrender to control. We were told where to be, where to sleep, what to read, and so on. There wasn't a lot of room for overthinking our relationships. We walked into our dorm room for the first time eager to see who had been chosen for us (providence). As grown-ups, we fight against providence. We champion our right to choose. But in the choosing, we also lose something. We lose the magic and mystery of having to make it work.

So how do we step into the thing we're not in a position to experience?

We certainly don't find what we're looking for sitting in a crowded auditorium on a Sunday morning. And community certainly isn't discovered through a screen while we engage in virtual living. We are made for more. You are made for God and for people. Every day and week and season of life is one more opportunity to open up our hearts, set them on the table of community, and invite others to feast on what God is doing around us.

In the following pages, I'd like to describe what the family of God looks like, what it does together in close quarters. Not in rows, clean and ordered. But life together that is messy and beautiful and creative. I'd like to talk about what life feels like, hurts like, sends like, cries like, and corrects like—in community. But mostly I want you to discover what it means to enjoy life and God together with the people God has placed around you.

It's helpful to remind ourselves that God's work in us isn't necessarily relegated to a church small group or organized bible study. But I've found that this is where real community often begins—around the common need of grace. Don't just stay in the bible study, let it become more. Don't settle for Sunday School when Mondays and Tuesdays and Wednesdays are available for more. The invitation of this journey is two-fold: First, take courage to fill your house, your home, your apartment with other people. We're not talking about a party—more noise will not placate your need for deep relationship. We're talking about opening the door of our lives and home to a handful of men and women who also sense the need for more. Second, do the work of getting your own heart and life ready to receive the very people God is preparing to place in your life.

Because mnemonic devices are helpful as we learn something new, picture community as the house you live in. Most of life happens in our homes—not that life doesn't happen on the subway or in the office or in a pub. But life that matters, deep life, happens where you eat, sleep, rest, and play. Each successive room we consider will represent an aspect of ever-deepening community that has the potential to be meaningful in ways we hadn't even thought of. We will begin in the foyer because that is where every new friendship begins, and we will end in the bedroom, because that is the place of ultimate intimacy. Each room in between fits together to make up a home of beautiful community. Your home is the metaphor and picture of your life.

Take a step of faith toward deep, fulfilling life together. Fill your life with the people that God has prepared for you, and work toward the goal of never again doing life alone.

2

The Foyer is for Introductions

THE LIFE OF DEEP community begins in the foyer of your home. Or as my grandmother called it, the foy-yay. In most homes, a foyer is small. And it should be. A foyer is made for introductions. It's the staging area for new relationships. But it can also be a place of awkwardness, especially as we meet new people and begin new relationships. The foyer is the place where people both enter and exit a home, a reminder that all things begin and all things end. Even relationships. The first step into a new relationship whispers to us that community is not an end goal, not a final chapter to a long book, but rather a thread woven through every part of our lives.

Recently, I was invited to a friend's dinner party. I was a little nervous because I didn't know anyone except the host. The closer I drove to my friend's home, the more I could feel my blood pressure rising. What was I walking into? Was I going to have chemistry with anyone? Was this going to be two hours of small talk? Was it going to get political? My nervousness turned into tangible fear. I was starting to sweat. This struck me as a little strange because of what I do. As a pastor, I meet hundreds of people every week on Sundays—I shake hands, hug necks, console hurting families. I don't think twice about engaging people on these days. Why was I having such a freak out right now? It occurred to me that the difference between my Sunday interactions and what I expected at the dinner party had to do with control. Most Sundays I know what's going to happen. At our staff meeting on Mondays we settle what songs we're singing, what I'll be preaching, and how we want to end the gathering. While there is always a question mark about how God's Spirit will intersect our plans, we generally know how things will play out.

As I was walking into my friend's home, I had none of those assurances. No firm expectations, no exit plan, no friends to speak of. All I had was a big question mark about what might happen. As I walked up to the door, I had to decide in my heart whether I was going to leave the party, or whether I was going to leave my fears at the welcome mat. I decided to go in. It was a dangerous play. I knew I couldn't control whether or not people would talk about politics or puppies. (Frankly, I was hoping for puppies!) In choosing to move forward and check my fear (or most of it) at the door, I soon discovered that everyone else was just as nervous as I was—just as anxious about fitting in and saying the right things and making the party enjoyable for everyone else.

I find this practice of checking our fears at the door helpful for those walking through the door into the foyer of community. Not that we can ever truly leave our frailties and insecurities at the door, but we can make a deliberate choice to leave certain expectations out of our budding relationships. It's like a metal detector at the courthouse. The security guards want to make sure no one is bringing a dangerous weapon into a courtroom. Weapons have their place, but not in that place. In the same way, there are some attitudes that just don't belong at the beginning of a community's formation.

As I have written and rewritten this little book, I've had to fight the temptation to neatly organize how community is supposed to work. Something along the lines of A + B + C= Rich Friendship. Unfortunately, there is no real math that works in creating something like this. Sadly, I've thrown entire chapters away because after finishing them, reading them (and having other thoughtful readers and writers give feedback), I've realized that somehow I domesticated this wild thing. It became a sanitized sermon. Pious platitudes that only work among the self-righteous. And as it turns out, the self-righteous don't really want what we're talking about here anyway. If anything, this thing we're stepping into is uncharted territory—unmapped communal living. Messy, unpredictable, and often painful. Because of that, it's important not only what we're bringing into these relationships, but also what we're leaving behind for the sake of fresh starts.

OUTSIDERS TO INSIDERS

Jesus' invitation for us to come from the shadows of obscurity into a family is part of what makes gospel life so attractive. No longer are we alone, destined to live in an echo chamber of self-doubt and discouragement. We get to be known. In a family. Daily reminders to ourselves are necessary—we're made to be in relationship, hardwired for depth and beauty and transparency. And yet, how often we short circuit these serendipitous moments in which we have an opportunity to invite someone to step over the line into our space!

"We live in an age that has replaced compassion with sentiment," said Eugene Peterson. We feign transparency and openness, all the while surrounding ourselves with a moat of self-protection. Those who enter in only come in through the creaking drawbridge of lists and expectations. I know this list well. It is long and burdensome and always smells of Pharisaical wisdom.

> I will let in those who . . .
>
> Love Jesus more than their own children, SEC football, and life itself
> Agree with me politically
> Have the same parenting style
> Have the same number of children
> Have the same theological framework
> Go to "my kind" of church
> Have a personal chemistry with my family
> Live in the same kind of neighborhood
> Have the same vision for life

The lists go on and on, and the moat we dig to protect ourselves becomes so deep, so broad, that even our own drawbridge will no longer reach the edge. We end up trapped by our own standards and self-righteous grids. Ironically, the sanitized, sprayed-down expectations do us no good when our homes are empty.

A bit of self-discovery has happened for me in this process. It turns out that I like lists. Things to do and items to fix. Checked boxes on a notepad make me feel accomplished and powerful. I don't begrudge the list. I am more effective with my time because of the lists I make and receive. The problem is that lists in relationships turn people into projects—things to fix and problems to be solved.

I've certainly thought to myself, it would be much easier if my friendships were only with people who loved Jesus supremely or with those with whom I never disagree. All the feels with none of the pain. But lists of expectations to be met before people are invited in are dangerous because they remove the activity and leading of the Spirit of God. We begin to believe there is no longer a need to pray or listen for what God is doing around us. We hesitate to even enjoy an unscheduled coffee with someone we meet in line at the grocery store for fear they may not fit into our relational paradigm. They may be unsafe, we think. We prefer to include those we like or who are like us, instead of venturing into uncharted waters. With pride, we stand at our own personal Sinai and give our law to those who come close, not on tablets of stone, but on equally rigid and unbreaking platitudes.

We like law. Law is clear. Defined. We know who is in and who is out. Law has edges and clean lines. However, as we declare what is expected to those who desire to come close to us, we quickly realize that no one can fulfill what we're demanding. It's too steep an edifice to climb. A perfect friendship is unattainable. It's an illusion.

On the other hand, the lists we create are not all bad. We are made for order, right? And who says expectations are a bad thing? Like the Old Testament law, lists reveal in us a desire for more, a more that feels possible, but isn't nearly possible on our own. And remember, the law kills. When the law is all we have we end up white-knuckling every relationship. Strangling every beautiful moment because it doesn't fit within our grid. We measure our friendships against something that is unattainable—our own rigid regulations. Deep down we know it never works. How can it? But lists are easier. Less confusing. More predictable.

Our souls are made for something organic and free and hopeful yet we still lack direction on how to get there. In the meantime, we hold on to the list. We determine in our hearts that we will corral the right people into our lives. By our own will and strength we will cultivate a community that measures up. We will lay this communal law over new friendships and see if they make the cut. Of course, no one can. We hold onto a "you're in and you're out" community grid because deep down we're waiting for the perfect person to come along, not realizing that God has already sent the perfect person. Jesus.

We become like the Jewish people in the book of Acts who rejected the beauty of relationship for cold tablets of stone. Law and lists give us a measure of comfort, but relationship and covenant fill in the soul gaps we all have. Thankfully, the clean lines of law get blurred as our eyes become adjusted to seeing the world through mercy. The law demands. Grace gives. Lists and law thin out the possibilities. Grace opens every door.

Isn't that why we read books like this? We're desperate for God to open the right doors and create opportunities for the kind of community we know is possible. David and Jonathan kinds of friendships. Naomi and Ruth. Jesus and John.

In honest moments, we know we are more likely to give the law to others while offering grace to ourselves. Giving the heavy yoke while also standing in judgment of those who stumble and fall under its weight.

We list-givers always hold to a double standard. We would never hold ourselves to our own razor-sharp law. How can we? This self-righteousness we enjoy gives us a measure of satisfaction; however, it only leads us to greater loneliness. No one will measure up.

No one can measure up.

Those who even come close to our standards get pushed to the margins. All the while, we know the law we are peddling is a death sentence to everyone who God brings before us.

Modern Christians are not the first to create this kind of grid. Humans have been doing this for millennia. A little bit of updating, fresh language, and a sprinkle of pop-psychology helps us to say with confidence that we only let "safe" or "healthy" people into our lives. Pastors, those who are ordained to tell us the truth, will shout through a face mic to get toxic people out of our families. We nod happily because the words scratch the itch of our list-hungry hearts. We think, This guy gets it. These problem people need to measure up to my standards. Good church people erupt in applause while forgetting a bulk of scriptural narratives that say just the opposite.

It's hard to get around the fact that Jesus ate with sinners. He didn't just let them in the building, he shared time with them. He was fully aware of their brokenness and failures. And he loved them. Really loved them. Perhaps you might counter, But they were unbelievers, Jon! True enough. But the disciples weren't much better. These guys didn't meet anyone's standards. Fishermen, tax collectors, and zealot rebels were the men who walked closely with Jesus.

They were in community with Jesus.

They came from the wrong side of the tracks and a solid pedigree was not to be found among the twelve. Except one, maybe. Judas. And he was the guy who betrayed Jesus in the end.

No real religious training to speak of in Jesus' community. And who knew if they could even lead? I think it's safe to say that if we were in charge of choosing the initial men to carry the weight of a new church movement that would impact the entire world, we would not choose denying Peter, doubting Thomas, betraying Judas, and the lot of broken, insecure men chosen by Jesus. Do you know who we would choose? The Pharisees. Educated, elite, smart, connected, honored. Clean lines, good education, safe. That's who Jesus didn't choose. Interestingly, those most religiously astute in Jesus' day were those who Jesus had the harshest words for. It wasn't what they could do that upset Jesus, it was what they couldn't do. They couldn't get their head around grace. And so it appears that if Jesus did have a secret list of expectations for his inner circle of community, he must have lost it, burned it, or buried it in a tomb.

Once again, grids are not all bad. We've all had unfortunate encounters and even friendships with emotional predators who want to take advantage of us. These perennial wounders are often people who don't understand emotional boundaries. But we cannot let our fear of being taken advantage of or being hurt keep us from being known by others. This is the entrance fee of community.

THE GREATER FEAR

Joe and Patty made us nervous when they stepped in the foyer of our lives. I don't know if you've had the experience where you look around at a part of your life and think, Is this real? This feels too good to be true. A job that just fell into your lap; a season of life in which everything goes your way; a marriage that feels easier than it should. Amy and I were feeling that and more when it came to Joe and Patty. Naturally, we were hesitant. Nervous even. But not nervous because of what the genesis of a new community required. We were nervous because of our knowing inability to sustain it. How would we keep from shipwrecking something that was so obviously good in our life? How would we build a true community with people we barely knew and yet felt a true affinity for?

It's helpful early in this process of building and cultivating a community to see your own frailties clearly. Perhaps you already do. Perhaps you are keenly aware of your bent for pressing the self-destruct button on what you need most. Either way, a warning is appropriate for those of us who know Jesus, have logged time in church buildings, have repeated the creeds, sung songs out of a place of abundance, read the bible with hunger, or even served in a place of obscurity. The warning is clear: the gravity of our lives always pulls down and away from intimacy. We drift—always—toward isolation.

In some small way it's like living with our spouses for decades and no longer seeing them. We may pass by them in the hallway on the way to brush our teeth without a word spoken. Physically seeing them, but failing to truly acknowledge them. We know them at a distance. I'm grieved when I find myself drifting from God in this way. It usually happens without any active rebellion in my heart. I move from a position of seeing and savoring Jesus as my treasure, to appreciating Him as Father, to merely acknowledging Him as a doctrine. Drift. The contrast of savoring Jesus and simply holding Him as true would be like a married man who lovingly, eagerly shows a picture of his spouse, while another married man only shows his marriage certificate. Both are married and both show tangible evidence of marriage to the other. But there is an obvious difference. One operates out of joy and intention and the other operates out of historical record. This happens to our hearts more often when the sun is shining and life is easy. We drift away due to personal comfort, what David describes as the times when "the lines have fallen for me in pleasant places" (Psalm 16:6).

This great danger of drift that we experience with Christ also happens with people. We drift from person to person, from one shallow relationship to another. We move to the outside without ever knowing it. We become satisfied with the solitary life. It is lonely and painful and one-dimensional. Those who choose never to lower the drawbridge, open their hearts, tear up their lists and repent of their emotional distance pay an enormous price. We are relegated to crowded church auditoriums and empty dinner tables.

Inside living is something entirely different. Harder perhaps, but beautiful and surprising and filled with joy. And dangerous too. I don't want us to miss the danger—exposed hearts mean real pain is coming. Inside living means throwing away our plastered grins. We stop polishing the fraudulent images of ourselves because we hope to be known and loved in real life.

THE FOYER FOUR

As we step inside, we consider the cost of being an insider—the attitudes and biases we have to lay down and let go of. Distant cousins, perhaps, to the "sin that so easily entangles" (Hebrews 12:1). These are chains that keep us immovable, four iron anchors that keep us at the bottom of the ocean of isolation. We're drowning, and we're the cause. Let's unhook ourselves and swim toward the shore where people are doing their living.

In an effort not to handicap a relationship before it begins and matures, we must make a conscious choice to leave our preconceptions outside and in the dark. There are literally dozens of ways we push the self-destruct button in our budding friendships. The foyer four are unhealthy habits, sins, and seductions that keep us bound in isolation. We lay these down, not because we are given an ultimatum, but because this is how free people live. "Live as people who are free, not using your freedom as a cover-up for evil . . ." (1 Peter 2:16).

For clarity, this isn't an exhaustive list. That's not really the point. You and I need to be sensitive to God's voice regarding the baggage and biases we're bringing into new relationships. I've found these to be true for me and I'm guessing that they're probably true for you as well. But please be careful. I am not the Holy Spirit. I don't want that job (and you certainly don't want me to have that job.) This is a potential danger of Christian books. The Christian book industry, by providing well informed and often biblical content, allows you to simply read a book as a replacement for the discipline of listening and reflecting on God's voice and grace in your own life. Take what is written here and let it sit with you. Don't rush over this section. Allow a word or phrase or thought to get lodged in your soul. Let these ideas be spiritual corn kernels that get stuck in inconvenient places in your heart. As gross as that example is, that is how spiritual movement happens. A verse or song or encouragement gets lodged into a crevice in our hearts or minds and providentially, it moves us to places of discomfort. That discomfort often moves us to deeper places with God and people (Romans 5:3–5).

Wind Catching

Let's begin with control, especially since I've already mentioned my affinity for it. Nobody's fooling anyone—control doesn't really work. It's a form of social fiction, isn't it? Nobody controls anything or anyone. Just this second, a microscopic organism that has the power to kill you in your sleep tonight may be entering your nostrils. You can't really control that. Or maybe you're a vegetarian and you exercise every day. Your heart could suddenly stop for no good reason. Right. This. Second.

The Foyer is for Introductions

Still here? Good. It's not a happy thought to lose you so early in the book. I use these frightening examples because we all know they are true. We keep these irrational fears far from our present reality, but when we sit through a funeral and see a pine box at the front of a church, we get the clear sense that life is utterly unpredictable. Uncontrollable. And yet, most of the time, we try to live contrary to that reality. We exert a kind of faux control over every part of our lives. We strong arm and muscle our way into our preferred destiny. In the back of our minds, however, there is the sneaking suspicion that we're not really pulling the strings.

I admit, control may be the hardest thing to let go of, mostly because we like it. We've learned to wield it well. It has paid off for us as we've exerted healthy governance over our bodies and businesses. But control doesn't work in relationships, not in the long-term at least. Emotional bulwarks may protect us from heartbreak, but inadvertently, they keep us insulated from those who might love us. Tall walls and strategic defenses (ironically) become tools in a lonesome self-fulfilling prophecy.

Jesus reminds us about the irony of control when talking about the wind. "You see the effects of the wind, but you don't know where it comes from or where it's going. So it is with everyone born of the Spirit" (paraphrase, John 3:8).

Wind is a perfect metaphor for what we really want in our community of relationships. We want something a little wild, a bit windy and messy. Not a hurricane, not gale force winds that destroy. A gentle wind that rearranges.

About once a month I rent a cabin for a day to clear my head. It's a personal sabbath of sorts. No real agenda. Some reading and praying happens. No internet or work allowed. Mostly I sit on the porch and drink coffee. The cabin sits on a small lake which is surrounded by thousands of pines and hardwoods. As I write this, I'm sitting on the front porch watching the wind whip off the lake, into the trees, and up onto the land. Everything laying on the ground is getting re-ordered by the wind. Pushed here and there. I hear the sound of the wind. I think I know where it's coming from and then it changes directions. A tornado of brown and green is all around me. And then it stops. Out of nowhere, complete silence overtakes these 100 acres. Even the birds sit in awe of the power. Jesus intertwines the unpredictability of the wind to a work of God's Spirit. We can't control God's workings. We can put up a sail and catch the wind, but we can't produce it. We have no jurisdiction over the ways of God.

So it is with our relationships. When we lay down our desire for control in the newness of friendship, we're simply making the confession, I couldn't control this if I wanted to. I mean, I want to, but I know I can't. My control is an illusion. God rules this.

To say it plainly, we have to be okay knowing that our relationships will most likely be capricious. Unpredictable. Variables at play. Messy. Just admit it, we are an untidy people. All of us.

Please don't feel insulted. But this little confession of ours should open up our hearts to the idea that God is, more than likely, going to reorder some things in our lives as we intersect with his Spirit and his people. In other words, if things aren't messy in your life, they're about to be. It's inevitable really. The God who makes all things knows how they are meant to fit together. "And he is before all things, and in him all things hold together" (Colossians 1:17). From the supernova in the outer banks of space to the tiniest cells in our bodies—he orders all things. Toppling governments and the tantrums of a kindergartner are subservient to his hand. Our relationships are no different. Nothing escapes God's redemptive reordering.

This should give us a measure of peace. After all, deep down this is what we all want. No person with an inkling of self-awareness desires to bear all the weight of his personal universe. We depend on him who is seated on a throne and "reigns over the nations" (Psalm 47:8). We don't have the capacity to control every person's comings and goings and the relational roles they play in our lives.

I wouldn't ask my kids to do my taxes or itemize my deductions. It is beyond their capacity. Why would God have an expectation for us to order what is beyond ours? God's call of us into community is a call to trust in him for what we can't do on our own. And even more than that, it's a call to trust that he knows just the right people that will drive us to deeper places of faith and maturity.

Think about some of your past friendships. How many of those people really belonged? How many of them did you purposely move into your inner circle? I would guess that most of the really important people in your life just sort of happened. Almost, like, by accident. But there are no accidents with God (it's called providence.) He moves heaven and earth and every little detail in between to put the right people in our lives at just the right time.

Gratefully, God is more than generous to give us the relationships we want, but even more than that, he always gives the ones we need. And with heaping amounts of grace, he removes relationships we don't need. He accomplishes much of his soul work in us this way. Every relationship that comes in and then exits is part of God's spiritual formation for us. He may bring someone near who is pastoral because we feel wayward and lost. Perhaps a prophet or teacher is given to get us back on track. These dear friends are keys for us in learning how to live and love when the waves of life are crashing around us. They anchor our lives when we lose our bearings. Other friends pass by briefly and deposit a truth or a seed that will grow in another season. Sometimes we don't even notice these pedestrians until they are gone.

People are like the wind. We can't control who comes and goes. All we can do is receive and be grateful for the moment. We can put up our sails and see where God takes us.

Too Spiritual for Our Own Good

We also have to try not to over-spiritualize what community can be. I know this seems like a strange thing to say, especially by a pastor. Can we ever be too spiritually minded? Can we ever have our eyes too focused on God? Of course not! But that's not what I mean.

It is possible to have our spiritual eyes out of focus, missing the forest for the trees, so to speak. This is a fairly normative complaint from God to his people. Because of our natural arc towards control, we often miss the point of spiritual activity. We like to complicate simple rhythms of the Spirit and community and try to find the "secret truth" behind them. This tendency to seek out the mystery and clandestine knowledge of what gospel relationships should be is a trap. Early gnostics fell headlong into this pit, believing the gospel of Jesus was too plain, too easy. Simplistic, and therefore, incomplete. Surely there must be more, they would cry. And it was seeking the more, the ecstatic and romantic, that caused them to drift into outright heresy.

Likewise, we often can find ourselves on a relational unicorn safari, looking for the couple or friendship that is imaginary. We search out a community that checks off every unrealistic box we require. In the end we find ourselves embracing promises about community that, frankly, don't exist, or at least, are not normative. Best friends and bosom buddies and vacation pals are the goals of modern Christian over-spiritualizers. They complain that nobody is deep enough or spiritual enough or sensitive enough or (you fill in the blank): _____ enough. Books are written by these mystics with the Twelve Secrets to Relational Intimacy or Five Heavenly Keys to Unlocking the Door of Community. List peddlers, that's who they are. True friendship and community aren't cultivated as a result of checking all the boxes. Real community isn't a secret to find, it's a gift to be enjoyed. And yet so much energy is given to treasure hunting for the mystical creature that we miss the thing that is hidden in plain sight.

Jesus addresses this when he instructs us to abide (John 15:4). Abide. This five-letter command is the least sexy, often most difficult directive in the bible. It's the opposite of lists. It feels like a whole lot of spiritual waiting around. It doesn't promise any timeline or give a guarantee. It's the long obedience in the same direction sort of instruction. Just keep doing the hard work of stepping through the door. Come out from the cold. Step into the light. The door is open. Get in here! Hurry up and abide.

There really is no silver bullet for this communal hunger in our bellies. Community is in the main and plain of living with people. Pursuing and being pursued. The push and pull of friendship. Eating and drinking and laughing and fighting and forgiving. Abiding. When Jesus invited his disciples into a new way of life, he simply said, "Come follow me." The secret sauce of the kingdom is actually really plain. Abiding—with God and with others. Stay with people. Don't quit. Fight for who is in your life. Abide.

Not Quite Spiritual Enough

The pendulum of believing too much naturally swings to not believing enough. This is common among those who have experienced the pain and failure of going deep with others. Ironically, if some believe too much (gnostics) then there are plenty who don't believe enough (agnostics). The definition of an agnostic is "a person who believes that nothing is known or can be known of the existence or nature of God." Sadly, our lives are filled with people who just stopped believing in what is possible. Not necessarily with God or salvation, but about community. You might call them communal agnostics. They have—we have—become a kind of communal naysayer. This is an under-spiritualization of community. We think, maybe real community exists, but probably not for us.

It's really safe to be an agnostic of community. It means that no one gets in. No one sees the real us. No one is allowed into the fortress. The agnostic becomes the self-fulfilling prophecy of loneliness. Real community does not exist, they say. This solitary life, alone, is all we have.

The Foyer is for Introductions

And we shore up our defenses because we don't want to be hurt. We discover we are scar free, but also supremely alone. I think about my time as a communal agnostic and I must admit that it marks the time when I was the most miserable. To believe nothing is far worse than to believe in community even while not experiencing the fullness of it.

After I became a follower of Jesus I was invited to a beautiful downtown church in Fort Lauderdale, Florida. Thousands of people sat in rows and we sang along with a professional orchestra. We patiently listened to the pastor parse out Greek words for us as he taught us the bible. I certainly grew in my faith during my high school years. But I can count on one hand how many people I knew. People who knew me. This is not an indictment against the church. As I mentioned earlier, I love the corporate, gathered church. This is more of an indicator of the plight of humanity. We just don't know how community works. And so our churches continue to be filled with toothy yet lonely communal agnostics who love God, but have given up on the invitation to walk in deep places with other people.

Like the Jews who fell asleep to the promises of the coming Messiah are the people today who once believed the promises for biblical community and then, over time, didn't. They celebrated the call of community to bear burdens (Galatians 6:2), wash feet (John 13:14), live in humility (1 Peter 5:5), and embody kindness (Ephesians 4:32). But because they didn't see it lived out well, they began to doubt. What they knew concretely deflated into something less tangible.

Many of us wonder if it is possible to have a contemporary community of friendship and gospel endeavor like we read about in the book of Acts. With so much time separating Peter, Paul, and the disciples from our own reality, it does have a ring of fairy tale to it. Hearing that these early Christians "had everything in common" (Acts 2:48) sounds far-fetched. We watch how modern spiritual brothers and sisters treat each other and it's no wonder so few are in community. At worst, a sort of settling comes over us and we say, This kind of community will only be realized in heaven! Our scars and hearts bear witness to this heavenly letdown. We want to believe, but in what? What is real in this gospel mystery called community?

I find there is a dance between believing too much and not believing enough. It's a dance we have to learn and practice often. The music is calling us to a place of substance that is touchable. Mundane even. Dinners filled with leftover mac and cheese, meandering conversations about the price of gasoline, and kids bickering in the back bedroom. Spoken hopes and restful silence can materialize when we don't try to make something magical happen. Abiding is slow. Our perseverance into the everydayness of a regular Tuesday dinner with neighbors, when almost by fluke, we find ourselves in the middle of something special. These are unhurried, touchable moments. Heaven has not descended. No glory cloud around the crock pot. But still, it's supernatural. Abiding.

This dance also moves our feet to places of the unseeable. The intangibles of relationship are the "fixing our eyes on the unseen" (2 Corinthians 4:18). A community that is felt, not measured. Experienced, but not recorded for social media. We've all had those moments of a simple meal with the right people, in which nothing special took place, but it felt holy. They are the hard to explain moments that cannot be reproduced by formula. We've all employed the Seven Ways to Deeper Friendship principles we learned in that sermon. Most of us have read the blog of the latest guru who promised deeper relationships in three easy steps (usually with three easy payments). They're normally all nonsense and land us in a place of deeper disappointment.

Ironically, simple conversation, burned chicken fried steak, and open hearts seem too simple a recipe for community. Too ironic a place for God to come. And yet the whole of our Christian experience (and theology) is that what shouldn't have been the path of salvation became our redemption—supernatural experiences born out of natural moments. Bushes and boats. Fish and loaves. Water and wine. God seems to defy formulas. And yet the one thing we can count on is that he uses normal, earthly things to accomplish heavenly purposes. Things are normal until they're not. The narrative of God's story is that he uses borrowed feed troughs to birth salvation. Smelly shepherds to herald good news. A womb of a teenage girl to raise the son of God.

What we hold onto is this: God is in the business of breaking into the ordinary, breaking our rules, and building bridges to places we couldn't go on our own. God does for us what we can't do by ourselves, using what is right in front of us. And he surprises us by the simplicity of his plan to get just the right people in our lives.

We're ditching control because it just doesn't work where we want to go. We're leaving easy-believism and anti-believism because faith is somewhere in the middle.

White-Washed and Empty

Lastly, let's go ahead and leave self-righteousness outside the door as well. It's not allowed in this community. Of course, we can't control if other people come in with this burden. This house of friendship has to be a place where new things can grow. And thinking too much of ourselves stunts that growth from day one.

Self-righteousness is a kind of relational cancer that kills everything it touches. Even the word is offensive to those of us who know our great need for personal communion with others. A self (on my own, in my own strength, and by my own will) righteousness (virtue, wholeness, and rightness) doesn't know what to do but to draw attention away from God and to our own egos.

Our clamoring for others to take notice of our shiny exteriors only brings to light how empty we really are. White-washed tombs was a favorite description used by Jesus—beautiful exteriors, but void of life. Masters of camouflage, no one seeing what was truly there. But we know. We see. And equally painful, most others can see the real us too. They just don't tell us. So we steel our hearts and attitudes, polish our exteriors, practice our religious Hallelujahs, failing to realize how paralyzed we have become.

The invitation of community says, "Go ahead and come clean with your frailties." Those of us who are serial offenders of the lie of good behavior blindly believe we've got our lives figured out, on track and in sync with all the expectations of heaven. Deep down, though, we know we're just a jumble of fears, hopes, prayers, and heaps of insecurity wrapped tightly in God's grace. We can't hide for very long how cluttered our hearts are. If we stick around long enough, everyone else sees us for who we really are too. I can suppress my brokenness and cheerlead myself into better behaving for only so long. The hairline fractures of my heart become fault lines in which my life crumbles as I lead poorly, drive angrily, or wag my finger frustratingly and try to cover it up with religious hyperbole.

If there is anything obvious in the universe, it is that we have a problem. And usually that problem is you and me thinking we don't need others. Self-righteousness always leads to self-sufficiency, and it's a trap that leads to self-hatred. Self-righteousness is a disease that kills.

This sickness is the natural bent of our broken, sinful hearts. The enemy's promise that "you will be like God" (Genesis 3:5) still echoes through our ears as if the snake had spoken directly to us. We resist our need for relationship, with God and others, because of our own self-sufficient, self-righteous nature. The offense of this goes to the heart of Jesus' invitation to us, "Come to me, all you who are weary and burdened..." (Matthew 11:28). Sadly, we give Jesus a gracious nod and say, "Nah, I'm okay." What we seem to miss is that our worship of God—declaring his strength and sufficiency—is contingent on expressing our weakness and insufficiency. One without the other makes the relationship a sham. That is, if we withhold or deny our brokenness and religiosity, which is so obvious to God and others, we make it impossible to have a meaningful relationship with anyone.

Self-righteousness is the most obscene of claims. Martin Luther's confession on his deathbed illustrates the very opposite of self-righteousness—"We are beggars. That is true."[1] We are more than beggars, though. Bankrupt and hungry, but at the very same time, declaring to all who have ears that we are rich and full. It's silly when you think about it. We have nothing on our own. No righteousness to show for, not before God or man. We are only recipients of the generosity of heaven. Nothing we bring to God garners his attention. No sacrifice makes us clean or orders our lives.

Why is that? Because Jesus washes us clean, calls us children, provides for our needs, and invites us to find our joy in him alone. He is the source of all goodness and grace and provision. He is doing the heavy-lifting of righteousness. In some unique way, we show him to be strong to the world when we finally admit that this whole religious exercise is only possible because of what he has already done for us.

Every time we get proud of what we've accomplished in our own self-reliance, God calls us to look at the cross and he tenderly says, "It's already done. You're righteous, clean, and called son or daughter. Live well. And know that I'm the source of everything."

While our self-proclaimed righteousness is rebellion of the first order, it is also a bit silly from heaven's vantage point. If I came home from work and my children had cleaned their rooms, mowed the lawn, and washed the dishes (which has never happened!) and I asked, "Why did you guys do all of this?" If their reply was "Dad, we hoped to earn your love," I would tell them, "Thank you for what you have done. But your work will never earn my love." Their chores, as an act of payment, would be "filthy rags" (Isaiah 64:6). And in some way, I would be hurt and offended that they thought

---

1. Hermann Boehlaus Nachfolger, "The Last Written Words of Luther," http://www.iclnet.org/pub/resources/text/wittenberg/luther/beggars.txt (Accessed June 4, 2018) http://www.iclnet.org/pub/resources/text/wittenberg/luther/beggars.txt

they had to earn my affection. I would sit my children down and lovingly whisper in their ears that their sonship and daughtership is found wholly in who they were born of—they are Quitts. Born into our family. Their behavior doesn't merit anything. They are who they are because of us. At the core of their being and genetic code, they are perfectly connected to me and their mother. I would tell them that if they never folded another towel, my love for them would be unbreakable. If they wrecked both cars, salted the yard, and broke every dish we owned, they would be deeply cherished. If they spoke hurtful things to their mother and hurt one another, my love for them would still deepen because love is the only thing that changes hearts.

The revelation of God's love and unmerited generosity toward us is the solitary weapon of heaven that can put to death our self-righteousness.

So take a good look in the mirror and make the confession that you, like everyone else, are a mess! Thankfully, you are a glorious mess in which God finds immense pleasure. But no amount of spiritual language or behavioral box checking can cover over our desperate need and longing for God's mercy in our lives. No amount of spiritual activity, behavior, language, or posturing will make God love you more (or less) than he does just this minute.

Profound freedom comes as you are able to see the real you, the Monday morning you. The you before your cup of coffee. The you who is unvarnished and laid bare before the bright light of Jesus and the people who know the real you. It's in that moment when a beautiful confession is able to escape your lips—"I am a mess. I am a loved mess, for sure. But still a mess." That bit of self-discovery is necessary as you and I enter this house of community. Because if you aren't fully aware of how jacked up, in process, and yet fully loved you are, creating something beautiful with others, especially other messy people, will be impossible. Serving, creating, and walking alongside others who are as broken as you are is predicated on seeing that you are in need of daily grace from God. So say this out loud. "I'm a mess." If in your heart you're thinking to yourself, "I'm not a mess. I'm not going to say I'm a mess because I'm actually pretty amazing and I've got my life together." That little thing . . . it's called self-righteousness. Grace is the answer. Jesus' substitutionary death for you and His embrace of the wrath of God on your account is the anchor for living in freedom. It's called grace. We need it to come to Jesus and we need it as we abide with Jesus and abide with other people. If your identity is built around good behavior then it will never be enough. You will never be enough. And equally important, others will never be enough—they will eternally fall short of your standards. Self-righteousness will always keep you in perpetual isolation from other people, no matter how many people you surround yourself with. It becomes the lens in which you see yourself and others as constant disappointments. It becomes the confirmation that people are just too much trouble. Walking deeply with other people and covering over their brokenness first requires that you allow God to cover over yours.

Make the confession. Take a breath and say it out loud, "I am a mess." Still refusing?

Perhaps you don't wrestle with self-righteousness. Maybe the opposite is true of you. You're not sure mess is an accurate enough description of how devastatingly broken you are. Maybe you're thinking it feels disingenuous to be so casual with your frailty. Perhaps self-hatred is a more apt description. Self-deprecation. Low-esteem. The perpetual blahs.

Whatever you call it, the love of God is still the answer. You are a mess. And yet, there is nothing quite as messy as the Son of God leaving the throne of heaven to clothe himself with the stink of human flesh. He entered into your mess and my mess, so that we could clearly hear the words of life, "You are the righteousness of God in Christ" (2 Corinthians 5:21). Those words change everything. Not self-righteousness, but rather, God-righteousness. For you.

Still a mess? Yep.
Righteous by the grace of God? Fully.
In process from day to day? If you're human.
Ear attuned to your Heavenly Father's affirmation? I hope so.

The kind of community we're after begins to materialize only after we begin to be aware of who we are. More specifically, of whose we are. We are God's, made for community with him first and foremost. "You are worthy to take the scroll and to open its seals, because you were slain, and with your blood you purchased for God persons from every tribe and language and people and nation" (Revelation 5:9). In other words, we were not purchased simply by God, but for God. Linger on that reality for a moment. God loves you so much that he ransomed your life so that you could be in community with him. He is not lonely, but he does long for relationship with you.

I hope a smile is taking shape. You are loved. Maybe for the first time you're realizing that the God of the universe, who knows everything about you, all your baggage, brokenness, and inconsistencies, invites you into community with him and a few others. He loves you, and maybe of more importance for you to embrace, he likes you. The mess that you see in the mirror is not someone God endures, but someone he died for and cherishes.

APPLICATION

Stepping into a new community can be more than difficult—intimidating even. Below you'll find some opportunities to put some skin on this idea. I am hesitant to give you "Seven Easy Steps." Not only because I am nauseated by the idea of boxing in the Spirit of God in your life, but because we've already said there is nothing easy about moving into deep places with others. So these are only suggestions. Be creative in your own context. Look around. Pray for God to give you eyes to see others. Be open to unique opportunities that God is creating. Open your life to ways God is moving people, creating connections, and breaking you out of isolation. As you and I move deeper into the house of community, this application section will become more challenging, simply because we'll be leaning into more profound places of friendship that require more faith, more trust, and more grace.

1. Ask someone from church or work to go to lunch with you this week.
2. Attend a small group at your church.
3. Host a dinner party with five or six other people who don't know one another.
4. Invite your neighbors over to share a bottle of wine or a meal.
5. Invite a co-worker to have a cup of coffee with the express purpose of hearing their story.

3

The Kitchen is for Cultivating

MY FAMILY AND I love to watch those cooking shows where professional chefs are in a kitchen competing with each other. Each chef stands behind a basket filled with who knows what kind of ingredients. Bubble gum, muscadine wine, prairie dog flanks, and iceberg lettuce. They are given instructions to create a meal that is befitting of their title of chef. We always laugh our way through their predicament. We're convinced they are done for. Who would ever eat prairie dog? But in the end, they plate their creations and we realize those strange ingredients have been transformed into something else. A masterpiece.

As it turns out, this is what God is after in the kitchen. Masterpieces. "For we are God's masterpiece. He has created us anew in Christ Jesus, so we can do the good things he planned for us long ago" (Ephesians 2:10, NLT). Of course, we hear the word masterpiece from heaven and we shake our heads. Masterpiece? Ummm, I don't think so. More like charred prairie dog. Definitively disorganized. Irreparably broken. Unpredictable attention-seeker. Desperate. Certainly not something invaluable like a masterpiece.

The good news in this kitchen of community is that no one is a master chef. Well, there is one. But the rest of us are novices. More often, it feels like a sixth-grade home economics class rather than a place filled with professionals. But we're making something here. We are cultivating something of eternal value. And it's important for our lives and hearts that we keep creating new things together. While there is one master chef in the house, he has

THE KITCHEN IS FOR CULTIVATING

given you and me the run of the kitchen. He's given us a recipe of sorts, but he's leaving the cooking to us. The recipe is one that has the potential for the finest community and friendships we've ever experienced.

Like anything that is truly satisfying, healthy community requires several ingredients. And like all kitchens, some ingredients are on hand— always in stock— while others require a trip to the local grocery.

Some of our most memorable experiences with Joe and Patty have been when we've literally cooked together. Sometimes it was just burgers on the grill, but more often our kitchens were filled with chopping and dicing and stirring. As I look back on the beginnings of our friendship, I realize that the little community that started with the four of us was cultivated in the doing together, not just the eating together. For sure, we ate and enjoyed what we made, but somehow the process and journey together was of equal importance with the end product of depth, security, and mission. In fact, very quickly our families began to literally meet in our kitchen or theirs. Around a sink and stove, cutting boards and clinking plates, something was being cultivated. Nothing had yet been created to savor, but we were all aware that there was great potential in what we were doing. And we knew that if this relationship was to grow into something that would last, it would have to simmer in the kitchen of community.

TWO WARNINGS AND SIX INGREDIENTS

This could be a book of warnings. Kitchen warnings, in fact. Some warnings would be dumb, more-than-obvious cautions. The don't put your hand on a hot stove kind. Most of us would say, "Of course—that one is obvious!" I'd bet money most of us could write our own book of dos, don'ts, and bewares in the kitchen of community. We've got the relational burn marks on our hands (and maybe the stab marks in our backs) because we didn't really know what to expect when we stepped into the kitchen. I would imagine most of us now know what to watch out for. But let me mention two warnings that are worth mulling over as we get our mixing bowls out.

Don't hurry. Relationships, the good ones, take time. Lots of time. Microwaving a meal is just like microwaving a friendship—it's just not going to be very good, and it's certainly not going to be sustainable. So quit rushing. This thing is more of a soufflé and less of a Hot Pocket. In slowing down, we cage the temptation to say things like, "I've prayed about it and I feel like we're going to be best friends." Or, "I'd really like us to go deep together." Or, "We've been waiting for a community like this all of our lives." I know that sounds like a no-brainer, but we say (and certainly think) these things. So here is your more than obvious warning—let's keep our mouths shut. Be quick to listen and slow to speak (James 1:19). Enjoy the journey with some new friendships and see where they go. Quit trying to make something happen. If a beautiful community is created, praise God! If the relationships go south, mourn them, take a breather, and move forward. Set your oven to 225 for five hours, not your microwave to high for five minutes.

Don't Compare. Comparison is the death of any good thing, especially relationships. This is where social media is not your friend. For every minute you and I spend online, casually reading the activity of those in our "friend group," we are unknowingly comparing. And in case you were wondering, you lose. Every time. When we compare, we come in last. It's not even a contest. Those in your Instagram feed will always appear happier and more put together than you do. Their family will always look like they had a better Thanksgiving holiday than you did. Birthday celebrations look amazing at their house! How come we're not that happy? Guess what? They're not that happy either! They just screamed at their kids and threatened them within an inch of their lives and commanded a smile so everyone will see how happy they are. Or maybe they are that sickeningly happy. I don't know. Either way, that's not the point. Stop comparing. And for good measure, stop making other people compare. Stop posting pictures that are staged. It's not good for our souls to constantly create a false narrative about our lives. Quit tagging others on your posts with, "So great having lunch with my friend @JoeSmith." Is it that important that we advertise the private lunch we enjoyed seven minutes ago? A simple text will do. Thanks for spending time with me today. I appreciate your friendship. Do you know why we do the former and not the latter? Secretly we like knowing other people are losing when they compare to us. So just don't.

If the kitchen scares you, intimidates you and makes you rethink going deep with a handful of people, please remember that God has plenty of experience working out his plans for you and me in the kitchen. One of the most famous kitchens in the bible is Martha's kitchen (Luke 10). I've heard dozens of sermons about Martha and her kitchen, and I've always felt bad for her. The sister of Mary and Lazarus, Martha gets painted as the serial complainer and sad isolationist, the lesser of the two sisters who is trapped in between the stove and refrigerator. The anxious, activity-driven sister who never gets it right. This is her reputation even now. "Poor Martha," we all whisper, "when will she slow down?" Personally, I think she just liked the kitchen. She was no old maid banished to her kitchen. This was the place of her choosing.

The scriptures don't say this, but I imagine Martha as a kind, slightly rotund woman of simple faith. No airs about her. She has a sly grin, messy hair, and a dirty apron, and she's generous with what comes out of her oven. I like to think that before the sabbath sun went down, boys from Bethany would knock on her door waiting for what they had come to expect: cookies and treats and steaming hot kugel. "Don't tell your mother," she'd say. The boys would gobble up her gifts and run off without even a thank you. A word wasn't needed, though—her joy came from the creating, from the giving. The kitchen was her sanctuary. Priests have an altar and farmers have a field. Martha had her kitchen. It was a holy place.

That's how I imagine her.

I grew up in a non-religious Jewish home where we only celebrated the high holidays (the feasts of Passover, Pentecost, and Booths). I can count on one hand how many times we actually attended temple for our religious training. But when the high holidays came around, that's when I was grateful to be a Jew. Seasons like Passover were intended to be sanctified and set apart for others, filled with stories about Moses and Joshua. Golden calves and stinging serpents. But I didn't know any of the stories. For us, the high holidays were about the food. All I knew was that our family would gather at Aunt Cybil and Uncle Leon's South Florida home for a meal that made Thanksgiving look like a TV dinner. Aunt Cybil is my dad's sister. I'm hesitant to say this, but Aunt Cybil is a caricature of an old Jewish (American) woman. Short, loud, lots of makeup. But boy, she can cook! Matzah ball soup and brisket and latkes as far as the eye can see. I was in heaven. I couldn't name even two of the ten commandments or spell Sinai, but I knew that the Cholent would be piled higher than the altar of rocks in the middle of the Jordan. Food was love for Aunt Cybil. It was her sacrifice. The kitchen was the place where she worshipped and fed her family.

I imagine Martha to be a lot like my Aunt Cybil, with less makeup, perhaps. Loud and laughing and loving her life. She loved her family too. Her sister, Mary, was always the protected one. The baby. Tender and sensitive. Mary's heart was open to the wayward and frail. She was always the first to cry or listen to a traveler's story or stop at the edge of a dusty road to examine a patch of kalanit. Mary was the dreamer. Martha was the pragmatist. Martha cooked because she wanted to make people happy. Martha's kitchen was well-worn. People knew it was the place of welcome.

And then there is Ezekiel's kitchen. An ancient kitchen. A prophet's kitchen more famous for the apocalyptic visions than for the veal. In truth, Ezekiel had a single-minded vision of a kitchen unlike any other. If you have never waded through the deep waters of Ezekiel's writings, you might be surprised to find four kitchens in the innovative, updated house for God. (See Ezekiel 43–46.) This new temple was to represent God's glory and his infinite value for relational reordering.

The blueprints reveal four kitchens, one at each corner of the temple. I imagine a young priest coming in from hours on the job. Covered in the blood of sacrifices with muscles aching, joints throbbing. It turns out that doing the work of worship is not for the faint of heart. Prayers given and blood sprinkled and carcasses burned—somehow heaven churns by what happens at this temple. The day comes to a close, the temple doors are secured, and the weary retire to the kitchens. Portions of meat for the priests are boiled, served, and doled out to those who enter this kitchen in the house of God. The work of reconciliation, reconciling people to God, now moves these men of faith to a roaring fire and a priestly placemat. They have given, and now they receive. Not unlike in Martha's kitchen, the guests here find a place that is safe from unruly expectation and secure in God's provision. This is the rhythm of the kitchen: giving and receiving. Hearing and praying. Hunger and satisfaction.

We live this kind of rhythm. Not the dancing kind, the relational kind. Our lives are built around the push and pull of time and people and food. The bible and our lives are filled with rhythms in which we orbit. Six days of work, one day of rest. Four seasons, 70 birthdays, and 50 anniversaries. More specifically, breakfast, lunch, and dinner. These daily rhythms remind us that much of our life is ordered around eating. This is not a book on the theology of food, but make no mistake, there is a theology of food. God creates food not just for our enjoyment, but for a purpose that reflects the values of heaven. Because of this, the bible is filled with images and stories and commands that revolve around food. The initial description of the Garden of Eden includes ". . . plants yielding seed, and fruit trees bearing fruit in which is their seed, each according to its kind, on the earth." And God saw that it was good (Genesis 1:11, 13). The Garden, it turns out, was a place of food delight. After the Exodus God used food to unite his people through yearly festivals and parties that were so sacred that if a person was found to be working instead of eating and enjoying, he would face a stiff penalty, often death. Even the aroma that rises to God's nostrils in Leviticus 1 is that of roasting meat for sacrifice. Often the most important things, sacred conversations, and spiritual decisions we make are in a kitchen. God made food, in some real way, as a means of grace to connect our hearts to his and to each others'.

Jesus liked kitchens too. We don't specifically see Jesus at a stove with a "Kiss the Cook" apron tied around his waist, but we do see Jesus next to a fire, cooking for his friend (John 21). Cooking up comfort food, maybe? Or just cooking up comfort? Jesus knew that Peter had lost his way and needed some reassuring of his place in this world. His call to serve. His people. He knew Peter had forgotten who he was. Spiritual amnesia isn't uncommon when we drift so far. It happens to all of us. We get hurt and then we forget who we really are. The crow of the rooster seemed to seal Peter's fate, and he ran back to his old life on a boat. But Jesus pursues, as he always does, and waits for Peter on shore. From a distance, Peter catches a glimpse of the fire and the fish—Jesus at work in the kitchen—and the question, "Did you catch anything?" Like a crazy man, Peter leaps into the waves and fights his way to shore. This is perhaps the sanest thing Peter has ever done. Head down and heart weary, Peter steps into this makeshift cookery. Sand between his toes doesn't make this any less of a kitchen than the one in which Martha labored. Wet clothes and bloodshot eyes don't make this any less holy than Ezekiel's temple. This beachside kitchen is where Peter is restored and experiences grace up close and personal.

Whatever kitchen God finds himself in, he always uses what's on hand with us, in us. He never wastes a thing. He doesn't look at our past and say, "Sorry, I can't use that." He doesn't look at our bad decisions or inconsistent attitudes and shake his head. Down the disposal with you. He sees everything laid out on the counter and thinks, Yep, I can use all of it! I can make something beautiful out of this. God also has some ingredients that he brings with him to the kitchen—heavenly ingredients from his pantry. He says "Use these. Toss this in. Sprinkle that on." He invites us to use what's on hand but also what can only be supplied by him.

This is why each community that God builds is so distinctly different from any another. Every community brings its own flavors and spices and distinctives. It's also why a stringent list of dos and don'ts, who's in and who's out, just isn't helpful. God is building a people, and he's doing it from different tribes, languages, experiences, preferences, politics, and personalities. In God's creative nature, he opens up the pantry of heaven and he brings things into the kitchen that we don't know we need. Items that a master chef knows are necessary, but things that those of us who are still learning to boil an egg would never think to use.

I like to remind myself that cooking with a recipe is still cooking. I used to think the best chefs didn't have to use recipes. I believed they cooked with their hearts. It's just not true though. A baker can bake with all her heart but if she leaves eggs out of the cake recipe, the cake goes in the garbage. Every cook, even the professionals, know there are must-have ingredients for every meal. Whether it be milk, eggs, and bread or broccoli, brie, and bacon, there are some ingredients that are non-negotiable. This is true in the kitchen of community too. God invites us to create something beautiful and sustainable. And if we're only cooking with good intentions and lots of heart, it won't be enough. We need the basics in this kitchen.

Ingredient #1: Love

Real love, gospel kind of love, is an ingredient only God can provide. Not that we can't be loving on our own. We can. We can behave in kind, generous ways. That's not real love though. That's more of a southern hospitality and honing of manners than a kind of love that "always protects, always trusts, always hopes, always perseveres" (1 Corinthians 4:7). The kind of love required for a sustainable, graceful community is a love given from heaven. A generous love, a merciful love, a forgiving love cannot be mustered up like a forced smile.

Our own natural love is often contingent on our feelings or self-interest. I often see this play out in my own heart as people drift into my life who might benefit me or our community. All of a sudden, without even thinking about it, I cheerlead them, encourage them, and lend a listening ear to them. I "love" them. As long as they hang around and continue to profit me, my heart is full towards them. However, the moment they exit my life, my affections level out to zero. This is true to an even greater degree when people leave our community in a huff or via a social media rant. Love, earthly, human love, is not something I can give them. I don't have any love that is sustainable apart from God. In my weakness, I have other emotions I'd like to express towards them. This is why Jesus told his disciples, "If you [only] love those who love you, what reward will you get? Are not even the tax collectors doing that? And if you greet only your own people, what are you doing more than others? Do not even pagans do that?" (Matthew 5:46-47). This greater ethic of love Jesus commanded is not something we can strive for. We don't simply make up our mind to be more loving. While loving someone is predicated on an internal decision, love isn't an act of the will. It is more supernatural than that. We first receive God's love, and then we remain in it. "As the Father has loved me," says Jesus, "so have I loved you. Now remain in my love" (John 15:9). The key phrase is "my love." Jesus is giving us his love. God knows our love is faulty and conditional. Because of this certainty, he commands us to hold fast to heaven's love, the only love that endures. The only love that is perfected in Christ. Any other kind of love we extend just won't do.

This love God gives us and then calls us into spurs us to champion what is best for others. "Everything is permissible, but not everything is beneficial" (1 Corinthians 6:12) in our relationships. "No one should seek his own good" (1 Corinthians 10:24) in love. Christlike love becomes the defining mark of how we relate to one another. The love of Jesus in us moves us to "cover over" the sins and frailties of others (1 John 4:8). Love motivates us to carry burdens that are not our own (Galatians 6:1). Love seeks to honor (Romans 12:10). Gospel love costs. A love that doesn't cost anything isn't worth anything. That means love looks past our own needs to the needs of those we walk with (Galatians 5:13).

As Bob Goff brilliantly coined, Love does. God's love does. Our love—human love—not so much. Our weak-willed affection is a puddle that reflects our own defects and insecurities. Our weak love demands love in return. God's love is a well that we draw from to sustain those around us. Love that God gives is the foundation, walls, and roof for every good thing God builds. Love, gospel love, is a key ingredient in this kitchen.

Ingredient #2: Vulnerability

Every few weeks I find myself sitting in front of a plate of smothered, covered, diced, and chunked at the neighborhood Waffle House. Not a healthy diet, but it's a regular appointment I keep with my accountability partner, Ben. We eat, talk, laugh, and pray. There is almost never a surprise sin or a bombshell that requires a third cup of coffee. We are generally aware of each other's lives, frailties, and the things we are making war against. When the last bit of raisin toast is eaten and the Amen is spoken, we walk away knowing something has happened. You might ask, "What has actually happened?" For sure, our friendship has deepened. Certainly, we obeyed God in confessing our sins to one another. Prayers rose through the smoke-stained ceiling above the grill and punctuated heaven's chorus. On the surface we scheduled a time for growth and spiritual weed pulling and left a bit healthier than we arrived.

But what really happens in these moments? Vulnerability happens—a necessary ingredient to cultivating deep community. Ben shares about places of brokenness, like a confessional booth, and then waits for me to respond. I speak into what I see and hear. I try to ask the right questions. It's hard to know if I do. He listens and I can tell he is processing hard things. He then waits for me to unload my sins, inconsistencies in my marriage, and failures with my kids. He nods and responds with a word of encouragement, or sometimes a firm word of correction. Maybe a verse he has been mulling over. I listen, knowing that I am being shepherded. This stuff is for the mature or for those who hope to grow toward maturity. We drive away from our regularly scheduled time knowing heaven has sprinkled necessary seasoning on our hearts. I am afraid to let too much time pass between our meetings. My heart is prone to grow cold and unreceptive to another's voice. Vulnerability is what I know I need.

I find this to be true in most areas of life. I want my marriage to be full of romance, but I don't want to be romantic. I want to have a deep soul, but I don't want to allow God into deep places. I want the impact of the Apostle Paul, but I don't want his suffering. I want the compassion of Mother Teresa, but I don't want to be around the dying. I want to have people see me, the real me, and love me in spite of what they know, but I hesitate to do what it takes to expose my heart.

The Kitchen is for Cultivating

As I mentioned earlier, my wife and I have had a group of people meeting in our home for many years. The original intention was to create the kind of community we're talking about here. I dreamed of something akin to what Francis and Edith Schaeffer had in L'Abri. A place of rest and peace and wholeness. A destination for the weary. Romantic notions all around.

Even now my wife dreams of a commune. Or at the very least a small neighborhood of homes in which our community lives together and cooks together and shares our lives together.

We started by simply opening up our home once a week for dinner and conversation. The romance disappeared quickly and what replaced it was something entirely other—work. This thing began to cost us. I had no idea how much it would cost me until later.

While the idea of vulnerability was fresh on my mind, I couldn't seem to make that gel with real life insecurities, pain, and evangelical suspicion. Frankly, I was afraid, and felt unequipped to curate a community like this. But we kept meeting. Kept eating. Kept bearing our hearts in ways that demanded a response. Truth be told, I am still often afraid when we gather. Because if there is anyone who is most aware of how inconsistent and fractured I am, it's me. I'm embarrassed to think I have walked with this community of friends and neighbors for years, and yet I am still hesitant to say that I need prayer or need help in my marriage or require wisdom about my vocation.

It wasn't until I was able to share my infidelity with them that I knew we had something special. Not infidelity with my wife, but with our church. I had been unfaithful to these people. For years, in fact. For all practical purposes, this is the sin of pastors—our scarlet letter. We love our churches, but allow our hearts to become discontent. We let our eyes wander to greener pastures. Bigger churches; better churches (we think.) It's pastoral cheating. It begins with what I call pastor porn—websites designed for pastors who are seeking employment. There's nothing inherently sinful in these sites. Yet when I am unhappy or disengaged or generally bored with ministry, fantasy is what I begin to seek. I know deep down that I'm not particularly interested in moving or starting over, so I convince myself that fantasizing about other churches isn't that dangerous. Pastor Porn[1]. I confessed to my

---

1. If you're not a pastor, I know this seems silly. But I've found that most people, no matter what profession they are in, dream about greener pastures.

little community that on many Monday mornings I find myself scrolling through those help wanted ads and imagining myself there. I daydream about how much easier or more enjoyable or more engaged the people are at Fairytale Church in Anywhere, USA. I smile at the thought of a larger stage and conference invitations. However, every time I turn off the computer, I have the same feeling I'd have with actual porn infidelity—shame, hopelessness, guilt. I knew I needed to bring this sin into the light. So I confessed. I was embarrassed telling these people how unhappy I was. They understood, but they also asked me why. They probed the interior, as painful as it was, to draw me back into reality. I can't tell you how free I felt when I unloaded on my community. But what if that's all I did? What if I wanted to get this burden off my chest but I wasn't willing to receive the kind of grace that called me back from the edge and into a place of wholeness and contentment?

We put on a pedestal those who are emotionally honest without embracing candid accountability. Authenticity appears heroic because the dirty laundry has been aired. Everyone in earshot thinks to themselves, "Wow, they struggle and fail just like I do. I feel safe." The problem with authenticity alone is that it requires zero change. It looks and sounds courageous, but is nothing more than self-pity on display. Brokenness, addiction, and explosive anger become badges that we wear when we want to be championed as authentic heroes, but we have no intention of asking for God's grace to change.

Vulnerability, on the other hand, carries with it a directive. As men, women, and families begin to walk together in deep relationship, simply connecting with our weakness is not the goal. Yes, we want to hear about each other's hurts and failures. But a kind "I've been there too," isn't very kind. The real goal is revealing frailty and sin so that substantive transformation, by the grace of God, can begin.

Make no mistake, authenticity looks very similar to vulnerability. It tastes like it. When seasoning community with vulnerability, it would be an easy mistake to pick up and shake a little authenticity instead. But the two are undeniably not the same ingredient. Before I undercut the virtue of being authentic, I need to clarify that there is a lot of good to say about those who pursue authenticity. It's the practice of being relationally transparent. What you see is what you get. No games and no confusion. I really appreciate those who practice authenticity. It's a good start. In fact, authenticity is required for vulnerability to happen in healthy relationships. But you don't want to cook with authenticity in this kitchen. It's an imitation. It's not quite the real thing. It looks and smells like vulnerability, but it's not.

If we want real, authentic, vulnerability in community, then it comes at a cost. It's expensive and sometimes painful. It often takes years to develop. But what we get is something that is worth having. Vulnerability is everything that authenticity is, but so much more. Those who practice vulnerability lay their hurts, wounds, sins, and rights on the table. Humbly dragging our junk into the light is where we begin. Then vulnerability does something courageous. It gives permission to those who are walking alongside to speak into the broken places. Sometimes a word of encouragement is spoken and other times a word of correction is offered. Either way, what separates authenticity from vulnerability is the invitation to others to get involved, to spur us on to Christlikeness.

Ingredient #3 Longevity

Real community is the long road. Community is the incubator for birthing something that has real meaning. We all know the depth we admire in others, but the longevity and faithfulness of their lives has usually come at an inconceivable price. "Not only that, but we rejoice in our sufferings, knowing that suffering produces endurance, and endurance produces character, and character produces hope . . ." (Romans 5:3–4). Our spiritual heroes have probably spent long periods of time in the pit, in the muck and mire, and have come out stronger. Hours with God; tireless wilderness experiences; trust in God through endless, painful seasons. People don't move to the Hall of Faith by spending their lives lounging on the beach. The common denominator for anyone walking in a place of strength and growth is time. (And pain. But we'll get to that later.)

Jesus spent the majority of his public ministry within a 100-square mile radius. He lived there, slept there, built relationships there, and consequently, died and rose from the dead there. And yet there has not been a more impactful person on the planet. Staying, it seems, is a key to the deepest relationships. Leaving is easy. Packing bags and moving from community to community feels adventurous, but it is only precipitous to paralyzing loneliness. We are made to go deep with a few people. And don't miss this—going deep requires time. Lots and lots and lots of time. Putting relationships on a clock is never a good idea. When we stay, dig in, refuse to be scared off, it becomes a cornerstone in the house of community.

Coming Home

Every summer I spend a week at a monastery. I drive a few hours to a little corner of north Alabama in an effort to realign my heart toward God and people. By the time I go, I can feel my heart hardening toward people and I know I need a touch of grace. Last summer I got to know the director of the retreat center. Her name is Sister Lynn. Sister Lynn is a middle-aged woman who retired from a nursing career to devote herself to a communal, cloistered life. One day during my retreat, I asked Sister Lynn about this particular monastery. She explained that in her Benedictine order, each woman takes a vow of stability. The vow of stability, not completely unique to Benedictines, is a commitment to live in a particular monastery for life. You read that right. For life. This isn't simply a pledge to an organization, but to a particular people, to a way of living, through every season that this world offers.

Most people have a difficult time imagining doing anything for life. Americans used to stay in jobs and marriages and churches and friendships for decades. No longer though. We are bred to be impatient. We are a move on to bigger ideas, better opportunities kind of people. We're intrinsically afraid of commitment.

My limited experience as a protestant makes it difficult for me to wrap my head around this sort of vow the Benedictines take. In fact, Solomon gave us a warning about vows—don't take them, unless you know you can keep them (Ecclesiastes 5:5). This is why marriage vows and the like are so serious. But a vow to stay with the same group of people for a lifetime? I've never seen it done. In fact, most days I feel like I'm looking through a keyhole into a massive landscape called the church. So much is happening, but I can only see what is right in front of me. And what I see are men and women who seem to come and go from one community to another as if they are simply window shopping at the local mall. They get what they need and exit quickly. "Back to the real world," they say.

There are 57 women who live in this little monastery in North Alabama, and each one took this vow. One woman, I am told, has been there for 63 years. I watched as two younger nuns wheeled her into afternoon prayers. They fed her at dinner. I assume they bathe, dress, and put this faithful woman to bed every night. This isn't just religious talk anymore. These women are in it for the long haul. The romantic words of Jesus about community and doing life together have been given feet.

Isn't this what we're after when we talk about doing life together? But when we start talking about the cost of this beautiful venture, my heart gets nervous and impatient. I wonder if I have what it takes to stay. To endure to the end with these people sounds like terrible work. We know that if this thing is actually real, it won't happen simply over a coffee, but over dinners for seasons and years. It's not enough to just catch up in the church foyer. This kind of community isn't developed in weeks, but over years and decades. Like our marriage vows, the promise we make is that for better or worse, I'm not going anywhere. To create something good means not giving up, never giving in. "May the God who gives endurance and encouragement give you the same attitude of mind toward each other that is in Christ Jesus..." (Romans 15:5). Built into the framework of community is waiting and enduring because we know the best things take the most time.

Ingredient #4 Diversity

Imagine walking into a Wal-Mart supercenter for your weekly grocery shopping. The glass doors swoosh open and you are met by that sweet old retiree who is now a Wal-Mart greeter. In the most kind, grandmotherly tone, she informs you that Wal-Mart has a new policy—you have to choose only 15 food items to purchase for the rest of your life. That's right, only 15 items forever. She invites you to think carefully about what you choose. Agnes (yes, that's her name) assures you this streamlining shopping experience is the wave of the future. She says that not only will you get used to the limited menu, but you will begin to appreciate it.

How would you respond to the new policy? It'd be hard to be mad at sweet old Agnes, but you'd probably be outraged at the company. You'd promptly get in your car and give your business to another grocery store. You'd say, "There are literally thousands of obscure food items that I need. Maybe not today, but next week I might need turnips. The next week I might want kale. Frozen pizzas or pears. Who knows?" We all know the diversity in our food is what makes eating it so special.

This is the kind of attitude God has with us when we demand that our community look and taste and feel a certain way. When we insist that only white or brown people, or only those with a particular education level or political leaning belong, God cocks his head at us and says, "You don't know what you're asking for."

To say it more plainly, homogeny works against the beauty of God's creative handiwork in community. Make no mistake—homogeny is what the human heart naturally leans towards. Homogeny means sameness. We intuitively gather with those like us, those of the same color with the same politics and same socio-economic status. Left to ourselves, we can't help it. The spiritual gravity of this planet keeps us from seeing our lives from any other position except at ground level. Then God wakes us up. "Awake, O sleeper" (Ephesians 5:14). Until then though, we live in a state of sleepwalking, in competition with each other. Sameness makes us feel safe. Safe from the jealousy of people's giftings. Safe from the envy of others' natural talents. Safe from those who are radically different from us. Until we are made alive, awake in Christ, we spend our best energy as relational antagonists to those we feel most threatened by.

And then a switch is flipped in our hearts. Scales fall from our eyes. We experience the all of a sudden that is in the best stories. All of a sudden, or maybe over a decade, or in the middle of a providential conversation, we begin to see those right in front of us as gifts. Distinctly different from us yet equally as creative as us. We begin to operate with a new vision for what is possible with a house full of colors, backgrounds, politics, and experiences . . . with God's grace. I'm hesitant to even use the word diversity. It's a cultural buzzword right now. And because of that you probably already have a personal meaning attached to it. I'm going to use it, however, because there's not a word that better describes what God accomplishes when a bunch of distinctly different Jesus people gather together.

Diversity is not a new idea, of course. Businesses require hiring practices that reflect racial and gender diversity. Neighborhoods that were once known for closed gates have opened them up to new cultures and nationalities. Even churches that have been slow on the uptake in this department are sensing a change in the winds. However, diversity is more than sticking red, yellow, black, and white people in the same space. It's more than a corporate plan to look more colorful. The Jesus-kind of diversity that flows from image bearing is saturated in welcome—a welcome to a hungry world. A welcome into a home, around a table, into deep life. A Spirit-enacted unity that is energized by our God-given uniqueness is what makes our communities so inviting.

We're not after uniformity. Just the opposite. We're after a celebration of the fingerprint of God on each one of us. We begin to believe that everyone matters. Men, women, children. All matter. Democrats, Republicans, Green Party. All matter. Presbyterians, Pentecostals, and those on the fence. All matter. The child with Down Syndrome. He matters. The broken down drunk and serial Sunday school teacher. All matter. Gathering for a bible study with people who look like us, vote like us, drive what we drive, and live where we live is nothing more than a placeholder on our calendar. That activity requires no faith or trust . . . or work. But when we invite those so radically different around the table to eat, pray, and wrestle through life together, that's the thing that makes our gatherings unique.

Even more, what makes this community so magnetic is this racially and politically diverse, gender/age mash-up, all bound together under a single banner. Please hear me, our uniqueness and creativity isn't what we're championing. It's a dozen unique people all anchored to something bigger than each of us. The banner we hold high proclaims to a lonely generation, desperate for community: Family is here!

While this conversation isn't about reaching those far from God, there aren't many things more attractive to those who are wondering if the message of Jesus has substance than seeing God's people together, really together.

We see this intentional kind of creative diversity in Jesus' choice of disciples. A tax collector and a zealot were both part of his inner circle. Someone who worked for the government and someone who swore an oath to overthrow the government both raised the banner of love. Both of these men, in spite of their chasm of differences, were bound by the power of grace. Woven together into one family to put on display the beauty of gospel diversity. As Dietrich Bonhoeffer reminds us, sometimes we love "the dream of a Christian community more than we love the Christian community itself." (footnote) Sometimes we end up destroying this beautiful thing God is building because our dream is just too small, too vanilla. Too much sameness.

The kingdom of God is designed to be radically diverse, radically creative—all colors, nationalities, tribes, and languages (Revelation 7:9). Boy, we have a creative God! Perhaps if our communities, friendships, churches, mom's groups, and small groups all look and feel alike, we could be missing the gift that God offers us in this kitchen.

Ingredient #5 Courage

I pray for criers to be part of our community. Every year a few new people join our little band of community chasers and a few others exit. And every year I pray that those who join us have weak tear ducts. I know this sounds strange, but I'm not kidding. Maybe you've been part of the genesis of a new community. It can be awkward because people are getting to know each other. Our guards are up. We're still feeling our way through new relational territory. These first few meetings are like first dates. Surface level questions are ok, even necessary. Where did you grow up? What was your home life like? Do you like animals? What are you passionate about? Nobody begrudges these questions because we know it takes time. But somehow we're all waiting for someone to cross the invisible line into the deep waters.

We also know it's impossible to force it. I've been in gatherings and have witnessed someone trying to push folks into the subterranean of intimacy too early. Boy, it's not pretty. It usually involves someone telling their most intimate, tragic story without warning, followed by the long awkward pause. We all make side glances at one another. We start checking our watches. We wonder how we're supposed to respond to this guy who just unloaded his most tragic, awkward story as we all nibbled on coffee cake. Please know, I'm not debasing a well-meaning person who desires to lead out of brokenness. But timing is everything.

Back to the criers. These aren't emotionally unstable people I'm talking about. These are men and women who are generally in-touch with their personal frailties and are patient and kind in communal settings, but also tend to shed a tear when their hearts are provoked. I love these people. I find every growing community needs a crier. Two are even better. Every group needs that one person who has the courage, in the right moment, to cross the line. A tear is shed, a heart is exposed. Time stops and we know what just happened makes our gathering a holy place. All of sudden, hearts are softened. Others begin to open up, to share their own stories. A community is forming.

I put the criers in the same category as the brave Mosaic priests who stepped into the flooded Jordan and trusted that God would split the waters (Joshua 3). The Promised Land was waiting and someone had to take the first dangerous step! We need these people in our communities today.

In his book *Tribe: On Homecoming and Belonging*, Sebastian Junger writes, "Humans don't mind hardship, in fact they thrive on it; what they mind is not feeling necessary. Modern society has perfected the art of making people not feel necessary."[2] Junger is talking about courage that is formed

---

2. Sabastian Junger, Tribe: On Homecoming and Belonging, (New York, Hatchett

in the foxholes. In fact, he contends that much of the post-traumatic stress experienced by our soldiers coming home from war is not only the result of trauma experienced while fighting for our country, but is also due to the emotional pain of the immediate separation from those with whom they lived in deep, tribal community.

A friend of mine who has a PhD in communication told me about his current research. It has a fairly technical name that I don't understand, but the premise of his findings isn't too dissimilar from that of Junger. He contends that radically different people will be bound together in the deepest community, often for life, because of shared crisis. It seems that journalists and scientists are both shouting the same thing—pain, trauma, and watershed moments that require enormous amounts of courage to face form bonds between those who experience them together.

Culture tells us that lifelong community is formed by building on shared identity. Homogeny says that white, middle class, Volvo-driving, middle-management families will naturally connect with other white, middle class, Volvo-driving, middle-management families. But the research says something different. Take two very different people (white/black, rich/poor, educated/non-educated) and put them in a crisis. In war. Do you know what happens? Depth of relationship. Friendship. Loyalty. Love. This kind of community in crisis takes courage. An eyes-wide-open sort of audacity. The kind of resolution that determines on the front end of pain that what will be gained is worth every aching millisecond.

Experientially, we know this is true. This is why those who have first-hand knowledge of a shared experience of a car crash or war or the launch of a new company find they are bound together forever. They have shared a few unplanned, pain-filled, yet sacred moments. Anxiety, uncertainty, pain, loss, hope, love, and faith are all crisis emotions that have the potential to unite. A profound and deep connection takes hold of our hearts. Do you know why? Crisis binds us together, but courage keeps us together.

For clarity, please don't stage a car accident, funeral, or new business venture just to see if a friendship blossoms. At the same time, these examples should cause us to pause and think deeply about the courage it requires to engage in this endeavor called friendship and community. We can't (or at least we shouldn't) create crisis. We don't have to. It's coming. Life is often just intermittent breaks of peace in the middle of tumult. What we must

---

Book Group, 2016), 2.

do is muster the bravery required to open our lives and expose ourselves to rejection for the sake of what might happen, what could happen—what most likely will happen if we're with people. God will knit us together if we'll stay in the fight.

We can choose to position our lives in places of relational safety. Live in a relational geography that requires no pluck or inner fortitude. Some call these places the cheap seats. I call them loneliness. The other option is that we can position our lives and prepare together, in community, for the inevitable. What is the inevitable? Catastrophe. Disaster. Loss. Life will hit the fan. Pain will come. Our health will fade and the 401K will tank.

Why? Because this lesser known, less appreciated promise of Jesus is still true: "In this world you will have trouble" (John 16:33). In doing life on our own, we will face these same terrible realities, unaided and forlorn. That requires a different kind of courage—a courage to face this unchartered journey unaided. But it isn't necessary. We can do life with others. It takes a gospel nerve to walk with others, but we're made for it. So when the sun is shining and the wind of grace is at our backs, that is when we seek community. Because once crisis comes, it's often too late.

Ingredient #6 Forgetfulness

Forgetfulness is a counter-intuitive ingredient in this kitchen. In fact, much of God's complaint against Israel was their tendency to forget his faithfulness and mercy over their lives. So why do we need a sprinkle of it in our relationships? Mostly because when we get hurt, our tendency is to remember. We pride ourselves on our memory in fact. But it would suit us well to pray for a dose of gospel forgetfulness. We are poor in spirit, all the while holding on to our wounds like they're gold bullion. Inevitably, these invisible scars become hardened tissue over our souls that keep us from feeling intensely.

While it is truly an impossibility to forget the ways in which people have disappointed us or how friendships disintegrated overnight, what we can do is take a cue from our heavenly Father who wills himself to forget. "He will again have compassion on us; he will tread our iniquities underfoot. He will cast all our sins into the depths of the sea" (Micah 7:19).

We never get the impression from the scriptures that God is forgetful. After all, his very essence is infinite, eternal. How could the God who names every star (Psalm 147:4) forget? We do see, however, God's willingness to move past, cover over, and begin again with his people.

The Kitchen is for Cultivating

In 1554, the Archbishop of Canterbury was the first to paraphrase this idea in his speech to Parliament, "I am not come to compel, but to call again: I am not come to call anything in question already done, but my commission is of grace and clemency, to such as will receive it. For touching all matters that be past, they shall be as things cast into the sea of forgetfulness."[3]

Psalm 103:12 puts this truth in a different light, "As far as the east is from the west, so far does he remove our transgressions from us." God takes our sin and transgression from us. Not until the east and west meet will we experience what we deserve. Do you know what that means? Because the east and west will never intersect, we can know that God removes even the temptation for judgment. Because of the complete work of Jesus, God makes it impossible for you and me to experience what we ultimately earned. God's forgetfulness, his choice to not see what is clearly observable to everyone else, is our model for genuine, enduring community. Not that we never see, are unable to see, or unwilling to see, but we are choosing not to see in others those fractures and frailties that simply make us human.

I've found this to be true, so far, over my 23 years of marriage. Early on, there were real issues which both Amy and I sought to work through. Some were issues of personal sanctification (becoming more like Jesus) and some were simple preferences of how we live together. Over these two-plus decades we've done our best (imperfectly, for sure) to lay down our rights, forgive quickly, listen intently, and put the needs of each other at the front of our relationship.

Sadly, there are some fissures in our souls that will not be corrected until we get to heaven. Idiosyncrasies, peculiarities, foibles, oddities, and quirks. I carry most of them in our marriage. Some of these are part of our structured personalities and make up our fallen nature. It is in these places that forgetfulness is needed. We need blind eyes. As the apostle Peter puts it, "Above all, love each other deeply, because love covers over a multitude of sins" (1 Peter 4:8, NIV). It could also be said love makes us forgetful. Of course, the opposite is also true. When we dislike or detest a neighbor or coworker, we see in high definition their every failure and foible as clearly as the sun in the sky. We often rejoice in exploiting their sin. But love does the opposite. Love forgets. Love is blind.

We should be the most forgetful people on planet earth.

---

3. James Anthony Froude, The History of England: From the Fall of Wolsey to the Defeat of the Spanish Armada, (London, Longmans, Green & Co, 1893), 452

Not that people aren't accountable for their actions. But in community, we hold onto the promise that God's mercies are new every morning (Lamentations 3:23). Mercy makes us absent-minded to yesterday's brokenness. Mercy moves us past what we can see and helps us to perceive who this person is in God's eyes.

God uses the strangest ingredients to create the most life-giving communities. Moses and David and Peter. They were all messes. All case studies of broken people redeemed by the love of God. All pictures of people who should have—would have—lived secluded lives if not for God's grace. That's how God works. He takes what the world says shouldn't go together and he makes it work. And he doesn't just make it work in a systematic, mechanical sort of way, but confounds the nay-sayers by creating something beautiful.

This is who God is. A creative and redemptive creator. He doesn't waste anything. He takes our messes and makes them into something new. He takes our weakness and calls it a place of budding strength. He sees our addiction and proclaims it a potential ministry. He sees our fractured, rejected hearts and knows they're ripe for a transformation. God isn't intimidated or put off by our messes. Just the opposite. He sees a list of on-hand ingredients for a community that will be as unique as your fingerprint. Then he adds a pinch and dash of his own. His secret sauce, of sorts. Without his contribution, our burgeoning community might as well be a knitting club. If God's grace and presence aren't the primary flavors, then what we hope for will never be.

Application

The thing about a kitchen is that it's meant to be used. My wife likes to remind me that a good meal doesn't just appear on the table. It's a commitment to get a little messy and to stay until it's finished. As in faith, we fill the kitchen with diverse people, take the clocks and calendars off the wall, and just see what happens. I find it helpful when I admit that our community is not all that it could be, that we're not cooking fast food.

Be patient with those you gather with. Love, vulnerability, diversity, longevity, courage, and forgetfulness are not only ingredients for healthy friendships, but also skills to be practiced as you gather around the table of grace.

The Kitchen is for Cultivating

The kitchen is the place we begin to see what life together could look like if God gets his way. If he can take our frailties and the few good intentions we have, and add in huge measures of grace, anything is possible. Remember, as you and I move deeper into the rooms of community, God asks more of us, from us. He reminds us that community requires greater trust, deeper generosity, and endless patience. We're not going to nail this all the time. But he moves us towards it anyway. Why? As he knits us together in a family, he also does the painful work of making us whole. The way in which we become more Christlike is found in the mess of life, with each other. Trust that God is leading you. Lean in to his grace. Hold on to the truth that he won't waste any failure and frailty you have.

1. Journal about how God has made you different from anyone else in your life. This may be difficult for you, but take the time to put down on paper why you matter.

2. Invite a friend to lunch with the intention of sharing an area in which you have failed and experienced real shame. Invite him or her into your story.

3. Cook a meal together with those you are beginning to walk with. Not a potluck. Literally, cook together. Talk about the challenges and beauty of having so many personalities, temperaments, and preferences in the kitchen.

4. Set up a dinner between you and three others. Challenge yourself by hosting two of different races.

5. Share with your community why and where you have a hard time making a long-term commitment.

4

The Dining Room is for Depth

MORE THAN ONCE AS a child I sat in our family dining room and choked down my mother's pork chops. My mother did not have an aptitude for the culinary arts. Actually, she was a terrible cook. (Sorry, Mom!) Most weeknights we simply endured her nightly "gift" to us and ate it with a smile, knowing she loved us. But then there were her pork chops. Oh boy. Burned rubber with the scent of diesel fuel. I would sit at the table as a twelve-year-old and think terrible thoughts like, "This poor pig who gave his life for us would be rolling over in his pig pen if he knew how poorly my mother had dishonored his memory!" By the time I discovered my pre-teen voice, I regularly communicated my disregard for mom's cooking. My stepdad, guarding the honor of my mother, declared that I would eat every bite of the pork chop. At first, I touted my sovereign rights as a 12- year-old. "You can't make me!" Threats of grounding, spankings, and the like crushed my little independence and I eventually relented. I can still hear the words echoing in my ears, "You're not getting up from this table until you've finished every bite."

The dining room in the house of community has the potential to redeem the ought to, need to, you're not getting up from this table kind of attitude when it comes to deep relationships. Community, for many, has become a thing to endure—relational broccoli, as it were. We dutifully chew and swallow with smiles on our faces because we know these people are ultimately good for us. The thing is, we know that we need to go deep with a few people. We know that we ought to carve out significant time for this thing our souls are made for. We know that being known in our deepest, inward parts is healthy and mature.

At the same time, we know sitting at this table will test every bit of patience and endurance we might muster. Sometimes we stay. Other times we push our chairs back and exit. We move on to easier, more palatable relationships that don't require so much. I'm sad by how many times I've marched out of the dining room, calling it quits.

WHEN WE QUIT

If you are wondering if Joe and Patty are real people—they are. Not their real names, of course. I didn't change their names because I was trying to protect the innocent. In this journey of deep community, there are no innocents. We are all guilty of failures and relational abortions. I am. They are. You are.

Seven years of walking with Joe and Patty—lazy dinners, late nights, hard talks, deep thoughts, theological wrestling, crying and laughing and hours of enjoying the deepest community of our lives. We built a community around them. This was the real thing. Then it wasn't. This begotten thing that felt like a great gift from heaven was over in twenty-four hours. Even now we scratch our heads about how this ship sank. Were we that blind to relational icebergs? Did we underestimate our own frailty and sin? Did we put too much weight on this friendship, not realizing it would eventually crumble under the pressure? We didn't know. We still don't know. But it was over and we wept; like Jesus over Lazarus we were heartbroken to be reminded that all things eventually die. In fact, we didn't just cry—we ugly cried for weeks. We grieved a real death. We were undone. It turns out, so were Joe and Patty. We only know that because they are also our neighbors, friends once so close to us that both families sold our houses so we could buy houses that basically share a back yard. Yeah, I know. What's convenient one day becomes drastically troublesome the next day. Every time we sat on the back porch we had a tangible reminder of what we had lost.

The loss of this community almost killed my desire to take my seat back at the table. Mostly because I know that the dining room is the place that requires the most work from us. Or at least, it's the place where our spiritual muscles are first put to the test. The work of community is just that—work. We've already established that community is not developed with a come-and-go sort of attitude. No finicky eaters or relational foodies are allowed. Once we decide to stay, we then anchor our hearts around the confession, "I'm not getting up from this table until . . ." Until what? Holiness, patience, forgiveness? Sometimes just basic adulting is a win.

This room, this table, can be deceptive. We are apt to confuse the means as the end. God's grand narrative for you and me is much more strategic than a few planned meals and weekend buddies. His plans are even bigger than giving us a people and a tribe to share our hurts and dreams. His plan is to use these people, often unbeknownst to both us and them, in the shaping of our souls. That's a *big* job. God providentially puts these people in our lives so that our sharp edges will get worn down. We're all a kind of spiritual sandpaper for each other's souls. Jesus knows we've got sharp edges. We cut and wound in close quarters. Some of our edges are sharper than others, which is why Eugene Peterson says that "church is the most dangerous place." Impatience or imprudence or negativity or naysaying—they all get rounded off when we sit around a table long enough. If we'll stay.

Even in the early church, the table, more specifically the communion table, was the place that unified. The table called them to forget themselves and see those across from them. "Because there is one bread, we who are many are one body, for we all partake of the one bread" (1 Corinthians 10:14). Paul says it's the bread that unifies, not us. We come separate, but the meal binds us. There is a substantive kind of power at this table.

CHURCH POTLUCKS

I've always wondered if we're really doing church right. This book isn't about the church organization—pastors and polity and leadership committees. There are other books for that subject. Though I have wondered about the church. You know, you and me. We're the church. Individually, we are disciples. Together we are the church. Whether we're gathered or scattered, singing collected or sitting alone, there's no getting around those of us who have been touched by the grace of God. The fingerprint of heaven marks each one of us. But I've wondered for years if we're getting church wrong—the mechanics of the thing. I've wondered what a person, new to the New Testament, would think if he read it without any outside commentary. Would he take the ideas, the commands, the implicit and explicit practices and toss them out the window like so many of us have?

I'm not trying to be a trouble maker or dissenter. I've given my life to this imperfect family. But sometimes—lots of times—it feels like we've sterilized the organism in hopes of creating an organization to be managed.

The Dining Room is for Depth

In reading the book of Acts it's hard to miss how the early church was so full of life. Of course, we shouldn't be too enamored with the early church. They had their problems too. Just two chapters after Pentecost the Holy Spirit killed a husband and wife for lying. In the next chapter we see the church almost split. Acts 7 records the first martyr. Pretty much every letter written in the New Testament was a message of correction. This young church had its issues. And while this new community wasn't all rainbows and roses, they seemed to know that the only way they could move forward was together.

These early Jesus followers seemed to embody so many of the one anothers that have simply become background noise for our lives. Love one another, honor one another, instruct one another, encourage one another, forgive one another. Just a few of the 59 injunctions sewn into the fabric of Christian living.

It got me thinking, where did these early Christians practice all of these one anothers? Where did they regularly meet to exercise these spiritual disciplines? It couldn't have only happened when they met up at the temple or in the market. No way. There had to be other times where they regularly gathered, rubbed shoulders, and engaged in real life.

Do you know where that was? Around the table. "And day by day . . . breaking bread in their homes, they received their food with glad and generous hearts, praising God and having favor with all the people. And the Lord added to their number day by day those who were being saved" (Acts 2:46, 47).

In the early church, it appears that community was developed, honed, cultivated, and multiplied around a meal. Around the table. Not in rows, but circles. Day by day they were in each other's homes, eating and celebrating God's goodness. And then God did a strange thing—more people kept coming. More people were added to the church. More people were attracted to gospel living.

Acts 2 is a pretty straight-forward model for church growth. Step one: Unlock your front door. Step two: Invite people to dinner. Step three: Eat. Step four: Add more chairs. Step five: Repeat steps 1–4. That's it.

It's remarkable how God didn't ask these pioneers to do something new. In fact, he asked them to do something really old. He asked them to continue to do what they had been doing since people were on the planet. Eat. Gather around a table. God was inviting them to do something incredibly mundane and regular. It even appears unspiritual. But it wasn't unspiritual at all. They ate, and God infused their meals with his Spirit.

The meal became the ministry. As they shared life together, it then became normative to share their stories of redemption. "Let the redeemed of the Lord tell their story . . ." (Psalm 107:2). If you've ever thought eating might be your spiritual gift, you might not be too far off.

But what happened between 33 AD and now? It seems that the church, in its attempt to be more palatable, appealing, and accessible has unwittingly done the unthinkable—we have closed the door to the dining room. Some genius decided light shows, not casseroles, were the path to growth. Rows of chairs in places of worship replaced seats around a table. Ironically, in search of large crowds, the church has lost the secret sauce to deep relationship.

What the church seems to have forgotten is that Christian culture is designed to be a subculture. Subversive. Counter to what is ordinary. Not invisible. But strangely, counterintuitively inviting to a few. The church, in its pursuit to be accepted among the masses, has made the worship service the centerpiece of personal rhythm. We've anchored our lives so deeply to the large gatherings, lasers, lights, brands, bands, and the motivational speaker that sitting around a table feels secondary. It shouldn't be though. It can't be.

The worship service (isn't that a strange phrase?)—row after row of people facing one person using his unique spiritual gift. The worship service—the school for doling out spiritual information. The worship service—the multi-media experience of smoke machines and clever turns of phrase meant to inspire. The worship service has become a large dining hall in which experts slop spiritual food on plates, promising abundant lives. This is why it's painfully relevant when I hear church refugees plainly say, "We left that church because we weren't being fed." We sing a song, digest a self-help sermon, and wonder why we are leaving hungry. No tables in sight.

I don't want to leave this section before addressing our deep need for corporate gatherings. It is beyond helpful and healthy to sit alongside others to sing songs to God, to sit humbly under the scripture as someone teaches and challenges our preconceived notions about life. The large gathering invites you and me to serve those people we might not serve normally in our sphere of life. On any given Sunday we may sit next to a refugee, have the opportunity to hug a weary stay-at-home mom, or feel the wind of God's Spirit that is uniquely expressed in the larger gathering. We need the larger church. But it is not in that particular landscape where we are meant to live.

The Dining Room is for Depth

As we step into the dining room we become aware of something beautiful and something problematic. Beautiful, because God has brought a few diverse folks aware of their brokenness and hungry for community around a table. Beautiful. Problematic because a few diverse folks aware of their brokenness and hungry for community are now around a table. Maybe your table. There is a weight to what is happening in this home.

It's at the dining room table where a Godly stubbornness is now required. It's the factory worker at his machine determined to get his hours and receive his wage. It's the college student putting the pot of coffee on at midnight because finals have arrived. It's the newly married couple who are riddled in conflict and aren't getting up from the floor until something is resolved. Deep community is sitting at the dining room table with no other option but to lock eyes and hearts, committing not to get up until the work is done.

Community will undoubtedly include Bible studies, prayer, house blessings, maternity wards, funeral homes, children's plays, and everything in between. But the unifying activity of our community is the dinner table. It certainly has been true for us. We meet and eat. Often, it's a potluck of odds and ends—leftovers and the like. We've been meeting long enough not to care what is put in front of us. We're there for the people. Sometimes the conversation leads to nothing in particular. We chew, swallow, laugh, and leave. Other times, unpredictable, non-scripted times, someone comes to the table with a fractured moment from the day. The table settles down and everyone is now focused on one voice. Hearts are a bit more attentive. We listen. Forks are resting on plates. We're working hard to make sure the person is heard. Sometimes tears flow. There are no rules in the dining room except that you have to show up. Be alert to what God is doing. This is where the meat of community is found.

A NEW LANGUAGE

The bible gives us a sneak peek into the inner workings of the early church, which knew a little bit about building unrestricted community around a table. What we find are people who were so deeply impacted by the message of Jesus that the entire trajectory of their lives changed. People who were haters of the church became lovers of it. Those whose identities were wrapped up in religious exercise found freedom to live wholly by grace. Those who felt lost and driven by performance were given permission to simply "be" around the dinner table. Jesus' resurrection changed their spiritual identity. But equally important, it changed how they lived their lives among each other.

The lives of the early Jesus followers show us a revealing, frankly convicting, portrait of the dining room. If the foyer and the kitchen helped you and me define who we do life with, then the dining room helps us define what we do with those same people.

"They devoted themselves to the apostles' teaching and to fellowship, to the breaking of bread and to prayer. Everyone was filled with awe at the many wonders and signs performed by the apostles. All the believers were together and had everything in common. They sold property and possessions to give to anyone who had need. Every day they continued to meet together in the temple courts. They broke bread in their homes and ate together with glad and sincere hearts, praising God and enjoying the favor of all the people. And the Lord added to their number daily those who were being saved" (Acts 2:42-47).

A re-education is necessary when life shifts. Whenever our world takes a turn, we must re-learn how to live. The early church was doing just that—learning to live together on purpose. These New Testament disciples were unsuspecting students learning to live a brand new life. Their old lives were gone and they were forced to create a new way to live. And what this almost inconspicuous description gives us is a broad landscape. Like seeing the Pacific for the first time, we are taken off guard by what has been available to us our entire lives. These early believers were having to reorient themselves, not to a new world, but a new way of life.

They devoted themselves to the apostles' teaching and to prayer . . . .

Language always changes and evolves as our community moves to deeper places. From the moment we are conceived, before we are even able to understand speech, thousands of words are spoken to us and over us. Over time, our minds collide with the meaning of jumbled syllables and we begin to discover and understand the meaning of words. Life becomes synonymous with logos, the word. Words like eat, smile, laugh, sleep, yes, and no are the scaffolding for a new way of existence. And these words have an untold weight and move us to pioneering activity. Words move us to activity. Like a comet drawn by the gravity of a larger cosmic body, the trajectories of our lives are pushed by the new life of God's language.

When God speaks the "come forth" (John 11) over our hearts, a new life emerges and we're forced to educate ourselves in the language of the kingdom of God. The new language of faith, however, is not spoken in a vacuum. These words are spoken to us, and are also spoken by Christian passerbys who have also absorbed the language of the kingdom. The words we hear are learned and re-learned over a lifetime. And because of this life of Christian education or re-education, we become supernaturally accustomed to the flow and cadence of this new language in community.

Think about it. The most profound words in our language are full of nuance. Words that have the most meaning have a depth to them. A texture. Take the word love for example. I love tacos. I really do. I'm supremely grateful for the invention of these Mexican delights. My salivary glands go into overdrive when I hear that it's Taco Tuesday. I'm ok to say I love tacos. It's a silly example, I know. But I also love my dog. I love coffee, medium rare steak, and old books. I also love my wife and my children.

Can we agree that the word love is multi-dimensional? I would never put the love of my wife on par with my love for tacos. But I do love both. A word so complicated as love can only be learned and understood in the context of parents and siblings and family and friends—a community. Trusted teachers and companions teach us how words work and what weight they carry.

In the same way, when a person is born into the family of God and put around the table, there are new words to absorb that have a universe of depth. Words like gospel, forgiveness, redemption, adoption, and grace must be learned and voiced in community. Otherwise, they simply become definitions to learn or verbs to conjugate, only to be used in particular settings. Even worse, if this new language isn't learned in community, these kingdom words are sterilized into trite sayings that have no real meaning. They will ring hollow.

But God shapes his people with a new dialect, new syntax, new linguistic ability. And like any language, gospel language is best learned and mastered around others who are practicing this language themselves. We would find it completely normative to hear someone say they were moving to Paris if they wanted to become fluent in French. How much more then should we enter into community to learn the language of prayer and scripture and redemption? The language of the Jesus follower and the language of community isn't just language of little league and the rising price of gasoline. Our language is something entirely new.

Of course, we all come into a gospel community with our own language. We are firmly established in the language of this age. It is a selfish, crude language that finds its origin in the tainted garden. Words like rights, independence, mine, anxiety, hate, and fear dictate what we believe about ourselves, God, and others. So when we are born into the kingdom of God and invited to learn a new language, it comes as quite a shock to us that these two languages are not somehow distant cousins like Spanish and Portuguese. Rather, they are night and day different. Light and dark, in fact. The old words must be forgotten and buried in the baptismal waters in order that we may fully embrace the new.

Well Told Stories

The language we learn together is of scripture and prayer. We learn a new language around this table because we are residents of a new kingdom. And this kingdom has a distinct language. These are the words designed to be implanted in our hearts. "Out of the abundance of the heart, the mouth speaks" (Matthew 12:34). But God knows that giving us language is not enough. He gives us a source in which our words flow. The scriptures of God and the prayers of our hearts are joined together, voiced together, because this is how we speak and listen and respond to God and to each other.

Please don't hear this as an archaic suggestion to be more disciplined. Please don't lump this into the guilty motivation you've been pushed into by a well-meaning friend or pastor. When we learn the language of redemption, salvation, and thy kingdom come, we discover we are part of the communal currents of a gospel river. This language taps us into something so much bigger and substantial than we knew at first. If we misunderstand the language of God and the language of prayer, we may miss God altogether. "In the beginning was the Word and the Word was with God and the Word was God" (John 1:1). His Word is who he is—we cannot separate him from the pages of the bible.

Jesus is the Word. The Scriptures are also the Word. They are both true and the same and a mystery bound together. This is why rote memorization is not all we're after when we're learning the language of God. We can feel God and experience his goodness on a jog through the woods, but to truly know him and learn his voice, we have to come to the well-worn pages of scripture.

This is why reading, listening, and learning the language of God in community is so vital. Learning any kind of language happens best when we are immersed in the culture. As we hear and learn the redemptive stories of the bible with others, we learn and hear how God is building a people. If we only read the bible on our own, alone in our bedrooms, then the temptation is to read it with a self-focus. We tend to only ask the question: how does this verse relate to me? In reading it with others there is a very real sense of God's Spirit working among the many to bring a deeper understanding than we could have all by ourselves. Reading in community changes our pronouns from me and I to us and we.

As we meet together in the long-term, we then become eager to use the words of restoration. But it takes time and practice. We rehearse and recite the words. We wonder when this God language will sink deeply enough that we will begin to dream in this language. Soon enough, the words of unforgiveness are hard to recall because we have heard and spoken, so often, the words of mercy. No longer do we linger on the past because the words of grace are written on our hearts. Words matter. We find that life and death truly are in the tongue (Proverbs 18:21). Words matter, but the right words matter more. Scriptural words are the plumb line for our community, for our future together. Teach them, repeat them often.

The way this works in our little gatherings is by saturating our time with the storyline of grace. That is, we learn how to pray and we teach others to pray by reading and repeating the redemptive stories found in the scripture. Prayer and the bible are inextricably intertwined. Because we are God's people, we saturate ourselves in God's stories and that moves us to pray in a particular way.

To say it another way, the scriptures give language to our prayers. The prayers put words to how God is moving our hearts. Our hearts hunger for the righteousness of God. This is the cycle of how we grow in God's language. He speaks. We listen. We speak. We grow.

Abraham's story and Moses' story and Elijah's story and Enoch's story and the woman at the well's story all teach us how to pray and relate to our Heavenly Father. This narrative is God's, but it is also our own. We read, remind, and pray out these truths. God is a God of creation (Genesis 1). There is nothing he is unable to accomplish in our lives. We retell God's great accomplishments on behalf of his people (Exodus 14) so that we never forget that he goes to great lengths to put on display his power. We remind ourselves that God cares about our holiness and purity (Leviticus

16) and has set an entire narrative in place to show us that he makes a way for us. We remind each other that God isn't simply interested in tribes and nations, but people and stories (Numbers 2). We cheer on the reality that God has a plan to establish our lives in a good land as we make him the treasure of our lives (Deuteronomy 30).

This language is best learned around a table together. It gives us courage to pray in a way that we might not have the courage to pray alone. This, by the way, is a basic discipleship model. You watch me do it. I watch you do it. You teach others to do it.

This is how all of us who pray have learned to pray—alongside others. We don't learn to pray primarily out of a book on prayer. We pray because we have watched and heard and learned from those next to us. Hearing their faith gives us faith. Agreeing with their prayers gives us words to pray our own prayers. We have heard others voice prayers of faith and hope and pain—all rooted in the gospel. We have heard them quote promises and lay on hands and cry unintelligible words, and it was in the watching that we learned to cry out ourselves. Never has someone learned to pray alone.

I'm always surprised how many adults step into some kind of Jesus community and have never been asked to engage in personal prayer for someone else. Even more surprising is finding out how many adults have never been asked or invited to pray out loud for someone. These are men and women who can stand before their peers and give complicated presentations, but when it comes to voicing real prayer, they come up empty. This isn't for lack of desire, just lack of language. Lack of hearing. They don't know what to say or how to say it because they have not been around real community where people pray. They know better than to recite a childhood rendition of "Now I lay me down to sleep . . ." but they have no other options.

Because prayer is learned in communal relationships, those who have never been involved in community have often never learned to pray. This is one reason community must be a long-term endeavor—the language of prayer is meant to be learned over extended seasons with others. I learned English as my primary language when I was a child. But I speak a more refined, more insightful version of English in my 40s than I did in my teens. Language, all language, gets better as our understanding and capacity grows.

As we learn about who God is and his intentions for his people, slowly the coffers of our prayers are filled. Our prayer, rightly so, becomes an echo of the scriptures and an anchor into God's character over our lives. We learn that God can be trusted, he can heal, he will lead us, and he has all power. In turn, our prayers and language begin to reflect that. Tentatively at first, but later with boldness, our community of faith begins to speak back to God what he has been speaking over us. We can trust you . . . We depend on you to lead us . . . We need You to heal our bodies and our hearts . . . Nothing in this world satisfies but You. For centuries this is how the church learned the language of God.

GETTING RICH

All the believers were together and had everything in common. They sold property and possessions to give to anyone who had need . . .

Radical Generosity isn't fundamentally about giving. It's about discovering that all we have is meant for the larger community. Our understanding of sharing is really an understatement of what these early Jesus people experienced. But let's start there.

Sharing is a preschool rule. Before we were fully potty-trained, we were taught not to hold too tightly to our toys. But radical generosity isn't the same as sharing a broken Tonka trunk. Having "everything in common" is so much more than that. And frankly, it's the more that makes us nervous. It has the tenor of Marx—an edge of socialism. But this isn't forcible distribution, but rather open-handed living. Gracious givers, not begrudging benefactors.

Jesus reminds us of the way of generosity—"Do not store up for yourselves treasures on earth, where moths and vermin destroy, and where thieves break in and steal. But store up for yourselves treasures in heaven, where moths and vermin do not destroy, and where thieves do not break in and steal. For where your treasure is, there your heart will be also" (Matthew 6:19–21). Jesus knows the bent of our hearts is to hoard up temporary trinkets. In the deep part of our hearts we know that more stuff isn't the answer. After all, if we're not happy with what we have, getting more of it will not make us happier. And yet we gather. We fill our bank accounts and stuff our 401Ks with the expectation that we will get what our hearts long for. But even for those who gain the world, they find that it never really satisfies. This is why we have all met very wealthy people who are miserable and very poor people with deep reservoirs of joy.

When we discover that life is better with others, the stuff of life loses its hold on us. We become eager for relationship, for those who sit across from us to enjoy what God has liberally showered on us. And yet we resist. I resist. I guard what is in my possession as if it is a block of gold. Sometimes I feel like that little girl who is huddled in the corner of the kitchen guarding her treasure. Maybe you've heard the story. When her mother asks her what she has in her hand she screams, "It's mine!" When her mother pries her hand open she discovers a dead cockroach. Just like that little girl, my guarded treasures are seen as filth. Others see it first, of course. In community, though, my eyes are open to a greater kingdom, a greater treasure worth holding onto.

The culture teaches us to hold on for dear life to what can be stored away, sold for profit. But we don't realize that these treasures bind us to the grave. I'm not speaking metaphorically. Jesus warned that those who hold onto their wealth will have a very difficult time finding their way to heaven (Matthew 19:24). Paul warned his young disciple of the same thing. "But those who desire to be rich fall into temptation, into a snare, into many senseless and harmful desires that plunge people into ruin and destruction. For the love of money is a root of all kinds of evils. It is through this craving that some have wandered away from the faith and pierced themselves with many pangs" (1 Timothy 6:9–10). In spite of these dire warnings, we continue to hold on to temporary pleasures for dear life. This is why radical generosity frees us to see our stuff as something that simply flows through our hands.

And giving to those who are in need doesn't appear to be optional for the Christian—our giving seems to be a necessity in opening our eyes to heavenly things. When we share our possessions, even going as far as selling our property that we might have something to give, we hold onto the command to fix our eyes on what is unseen, knowing that what is unseen is eternal (2 Corinthians 4:18).

My first experience with this kind of generosity was with Mr. Davis. I was fresh out of college and working in my first church job. Mr. Davis was an older man in our church family who would often shake your hand and leave a $100 bill behind. It was shocking. He just loved to bless people. Before long, people began looking for Mr. Davis so they could shake his hand. He had enough time in this world to know that his treasure wasn't in his wallet or parked in his garage. He also seemed to have a knack for knowing who was in need, or even who would soon be in need. God would give Mr. Davis names of people and specific amounts of money to give away. Not long after meeting Mr. Davis, he gave my wife and me a check for $1000. We didn't know how to respond, especially since we didn't think we needed the money. We smiled and said thank you with a bewildered expression, and were confident God would help us see. Two weeks later Amy lost her job. That money was used to keep us afloat until Amy could secure another position. God provided for us before we even knew we needed it. This is what happens in community! Certainly God could have provided for us in more spectacular, dramatic means, but he chose to provide for us through his people.

Development of this kind of generosity is necessary as we sit at the table of community. Without a gospel understanding of the purpose of our possessions, people become burdens, barriers to getting what we want. They become inconvenient tasks to move off our do-gooder list. Or worse yet, they become trophies of our benevolence. We give so we can be seen giving.

Can you imagine a potluck dinner in which everyone plays zone defense on their potato salad? Hearing the word "mine" in this context would shock even the most selfish of us. No, we bring more than we can eat and lay it freely on the table. And in turn, we enjoy what others have brought to lay freely on the table. We are glad to bring home an empty casserole dish. A communal, radical kind of generosity becomes commonplace when we begin to walk deeply with others. Radical and over-the-top open-handedness is intrinsic to our faith. It is not a special or unique way we operate with those in need, but an overflow of the grace of God in our own lives.

Now before you claim that you don't have surplus to give, consider the early Macedonian church. They understood that this kind of generosity never flowed out of physical abundance, but out of the deep wells of love. "In the midst of a very severe trial, their overflowing joy and their extreme poverty welled up in rich generosity" (2 Corinthians 8:2). Rich generosity welled up out of their extreme poverty. This gives us the unmistakable impression that generosity is not predicated on what we have, but on what we are willing to give. Those are two very different ideals.

This begs the question. Why not just generosity? Why does it have to be radical? The adjective radical shouldn't have to be a distinctive among other Jesus followers. We are simply "little Christs"—Christians. Our lives remade in the image of the most generous person in the universe.

The type of giving we're talking about is designed to be normative in the family of God. But to those who are on the outside looking in, what we do with our money, stuff, time, and affections will appear radical, revolutionary, in fact. When we desire to walk in this Acts style of community, we are making a public confession about where our treasures lie. Gold and silver have lost their glimmer.

It's in the passing on of what we have to others that we pass what I call the Treasure Test. The Treasure Test is a spiritual exam we are given many times over in our lifetimes. With every raise or promotion or opportunity to rise in the corporate ranks, we must answer this question: What is my ultimate treasure? Often, we stumble into this exam unprepared and mumble the name Jesus. We hope that will be enough, but we know how we've lived. It becomes easy to see what we value most. Simply follow the trail of our checkbooks, debit cards, words spoken, and time spent. We must ask ourselves, What do I get most passionate about, most angry over? Where do I really give my all? Jesus would say, "That is where your treasure lies."

I can't tell you how many times I have taken the test and failed miserably. I followed the trail of my money and emotions and time and came to a throne. Do you know who was on that throne? Me. I was there ruling over my little life—my little kingdom.

Thankfully, God doesn't exclude me from the table of fellowship because of my bad manners and frail heart. Ironically, my rebellion and sin were spoken about at a table. A dinner table. Jesus knew what I would do. How I would live. And at that table he reminded his disciples that his body and blood, represented by bread and wine, would put me in right relationship with my Heavenly Father. Jesus' radical generosity on the cross, on my account, secures my place at the banquet table of heaven.

I'm reminded that my stingy heart in the here and now makes it difficult to sit at the table of community with those who have real need. God gently teaches me and corrects me. Loves me and reveals his grace to me in greater color. I've been generous to you. Radically generous. Now, do likewise.

His generosity moves us to a kind of giving that will confound those outside of this kingdom life. Jesus' words, "It is more blessed to give than to receive" (Acts 20:35), have an even greater ring of radical when laid beside the words of Malcomb Forbes, "He who dies with the most toys wins." This kind of gospel generosity will either appear as beautiful to onlookers or as a stench. While I have met many who perceive the upside-down nature of kingdom life to be asinine and foolish, I've found many more are drawn to the bigheartedness and broad invitation of what it means to belong.

Jesus was a radical. We love His kindness, compassion, and love for the poor, but we get downright squirmy when he calls us to something more than this world requires. Thankfully, he doesn't call us to this alone. Radical generosity is meant to be developed, experienced, and stoked in the context of community. Like prayer, we're unable to learn the joy of giving in isolation. After all, in our aloneness, who would we give to? Who would we receive from? How can we practice generosity when we aren't aware of other's needs?

When we sit in the dining room of community and look around the table, we see people who are like us—people who are perpetually in need. And in God's promises to provide everything we need, he has given us these people. While many of us are only in need of a listening ear, a tender touch, or a prayer uttered on our behalf, many others will sit across from us at this table with very real, tangible needs—food, clothing, baby formula, and money for bills. The needs all around us, and in us, are real.

In part, this means letting people in. Allowing them to see where we have a deficit. Otherwise our friendships are only superficial. Why in the world would we open up about our emotional frailties but won't be honest about our financial ones? Seeing people I have known for years declare bankruptcy makes me want to scream. I shake my head and think, *Why didn't they ask for help?* Why are we so prideful, protective of this little part of our lives? Giving people permission to see into all the parts of our lives makes community dangerous, but also very satisfying.

In the early days of our church family, Bruce and Stacy showed up and modeled for us what it meant to serve, give, shepherd, and live out the life of joy and generosity that we all wanted. Every person who was in relationship with them would testify that they poured out their lives for everyone around them. These were mature Jesus people. Bruce soon became an elder at our church. He walked in a quiet humility. You would never know, at first glance, that he held a PhD, oversaw a large company, and led thousands of people to Christ. Twenty-five years my senior, Bruce shepherded me much more than I shepherded him. For several years I did my best to come alongside, to spur Bruce and Stacy along. Mostly, I just thanked God that they were part of our community. Then the unthinkable happened. Stacy was diagnosed with cancer. She fought well. Multiple rounds of treatment and specialists abounded. But ultimately, Stacy lost her battle and entered into eternity with her Treasure. Our young church had never experienced a death. The average age of our little congregation at that time was 28. We were experts with new babies, but not so much with funerals. Honestly, I didn't know what to do. I asked other pastors in town what they did when people died. They gave me cock-eyed looks and said something along the lines of, "Pastor them, you dummy." I didn't really know what that looked like in this kind of pain. After the funeral I mustered up as much courage as I could and arrived at Bruce's home, only to find out that I was late. Fifteen other men and women from our church were already at his house. As I nervously walked in, one of these merciful women leaned over to me and whispered, "Hey, we've got this!" In fact, several of them had been there most of night. I found out later some had been at their home off and on for weeks. Keeping the house clean; filling the refrigerator; praying with Bruce and giving an ear to his grief. I stuck around in the shadows and watched as this community did what they were made to do—bear burdens and give deeply of themselves. This family of friendships was naturally walking in an overflow of generosity. They had created a natural rhythm of giving and receiving.

That picture has now become a defining mark for me. This is what generosity looks like. It's not the ability to write a big check and walk away. Generosity must cost us personally.

Bruce and Stacy were fortunate that they had made the choice to walk in deep community before tragedy struck. They loved, served, and ate alongside these people for long stretches. Radical generosity was second-hand to this group of men and women. Meals shared, money given, babies watched, houses cleaned, funerals planned. They were old enough and had enough bruises from life to know they needed each other.

Unfortunately, tragic circumstances find us in places of isolation. If we aren't already walking deeply with others when disaster strikes, often it's too late to develop community. We stand alone in our times of greatest need, not because no one cares, but because no one knows. So instead of walking hand-in-hand through our heartbreak, we are left to walk through it alone. We like to enjoy relationships when it's sunny. But ultimately, we are able to eat of the fruit of community when the storms come. So we see that it's often in the sunny seasons of life that we plant and sow, and in the times of pain and uncertainty we reap the harvest. Radical generosity is the fruit we enjoy around this table.

DOING WHAT NOBODY ELSE IS DOING

They devoted themselves to the apostles' teaching and to fellowship, to the breaking of bread and to prayer. Everyone was filled with awe at the many wonders and signs performed by the apostles...

This early church community gathered together to eat, a lot! I can get behind this kind of church, can't you? And as they ate together, the language of the kingdom was developed. A giving and receiving was cultivated. Eyes were opened to the needs around the table. Extra chairs were set out for those being added to this young family. It sounds beautiful and exciting. What's most striking is their devotion to the apostles' teaching.

With 2000 years to buffer our beliefs, it's worth reminding ourselves that the world was not so different then than it is now. It lacked some of our modern conveniences, but the ethos of Rome was the same as America or Europe today. Get what we can, while we can. This life is about championing our rights, our privileges, and seeking the most acclaim we can! There were tyrants and power-hungry leaders, just like there are today. Corrupt governments and annoying neighbors, just like there are today. Haves and have-nots determining who feasts and who goes hungry. Just like today. It is a spiritual principle for the ages: those born of this world have the desires of this world. And those born of another world, the more real world of heaven and Spirit, carry the desires and devotion of that world.

When a person is born into the kingdom of God, the soil of his heart is fertile ground for a new kind of devotion—a counter-intuitive devotion. A devotion that doesn't make sense to the outside. The community that sits around the table is meant to water and fertilize and speak tender words over this new seed.

There could not have been any teaching more counter-intuitive in the first century than the apostles' teaching. This new teaching was grace. Unmerited favor from heaven. What is deserved is not given. Rights previously endowed now set aside. Lives laid down. Forgiveness for enemies a must. The every-man-for-himself philosophy was crucified on the cross with every other vile sin. This new church was putting skin on Jesus' command, "If anyone would come after me, let him deny himself and take up his cross daily and follow me. For whoever would save his life will lose it, but whoever loses his life for my sake will save it" (Luke 9:23–24).

This new church wasn't simply proclaiming new life, it was demonstrating a new way to live. And to a watching world, it didn't make sense.

This counter-intuitive devotion means laying down rights. I don't know anything more counter-intuitive than this quest. Naturally, we want to get our way and have our rights upheld. This isn't to say we want to tread on others, but if I have to choose between my desires and someone else's, most days I choose me. The natural inclination of our hearts is to protect ourselves at any cost. But the counter-intuitive devotion of a disciple is to lay down our lives and rights for the sake of something better, something more satisfying.

We were eating dinner recently with our community when Ben happened to mention that they had to put their family's dog to sleep that week. We all expressed our sorrow for the loss of the dog that his family had loved for years. Ben went on to explain that his neighbors were dog-sitting for friends, and the dog they were watching had dug under the fence and attacked Ben's dog. The bites and injuries were severe enough that the vet recommended that they put their dog to sleep. We were all shocked as the story unfolded. We peppered Ben and his wife with questions—What are you going to do? Are you going sue your neighbor? Did you make your neighbor pay for your vet bill? In hindsight, it is clear we had all taken on a strange offense on their behalf. After all, he needed vindication, right?! Ben looked at us as if we were crazy, as if the questions we were asking hadn't even occurred to him. He looked down at his dinner plate and said, "We're not going do anything. We're in relationship with our neighbor—we've been friends since high school. It was an accident. I mean, I guess I have the right to sue, but I'm laying down that right for the sake of relationship—for the sake of what's better." Our group went silent around the dinner table, realizing that Ben had just called us back into reality.

We had been taken to school in that moment around the table. He had reminded us of how counter-intuitive this kingdom life is. He might just as well have been teaching the Lord's prayer to us heathens. "Your kingdom come." That's what Ben was saying. This unseen kingdom of Jesus always trumps the anemic kingdom of this world. Culture says, "Give me what I deserve." God's kingdom says, "You don't want what you deserve." This upside-down nature of the Kingdom of God reminds us that our little kingdoms need to crumble. God is building something far superior, far more satisfying.

Someone might ask, "Don't we have rights?" Of course we do. But as we walk in community, we learn to lay down those rights for the sake of others. Relationships matter more than what we think is due us. Jesus modeled this for us when he walked on the earth. He didn't come into the world to be right. He came to serve. Jesus never championed his cause. He chose a life of obscurity for the sake of God's glory.

This counter-intuitive devotion calls us to lay down our privileges and to pick up love. Not the syrupy kind of love that can be washed off or even rationalized. Not the kind of love that can be stirred up by a passionate song or a soul-stirring sermon. That kind of love won't make it past the church parking lot. We need a love that moves us past the line of reasonableness. A kind of love that causes those outside the Jesus community, outside the kingdom of God, to shake their heads at us and whisper, "That's too much."

Isn't that what we're after?

And yet, when left to ourselves, a sensible and rational kind of faith takes our hearts captive. We don't want to live too radically. Not too much, we say. Just enough Jesus to get us to heaven. Just enough love to set us apart from the atheist or white supremacist. But not too much! We don't want to be kooky, overbearing, or hyper-spiritual. We never want to make those around us uncomfortable with our Jesus.

Oh, how we need a revival of love in our hearts! Something crazy. We have grown cold when our fear of others stands above our love for God and for his people. Personal respectability and pride have clogged up deep reservoirs that were made for rivers of love. We have become comfortable with empty, cold hearts. We have settled for pleasantries and spiritual language instead of the white-hotness that comes from being overcome by God's goodness. But not love.

This is why we have to sit around the table of community where we push each other to this kind of passion. A kind of violence is required to move us from the position of level-headed thinking and into a this is what I was made for kind of radical living. Gently and persistently, often with tears, community is meant to be the impetus to more. Love is the more. Love is what we're after. Love is the aim of our lives. Love is the alms we give to the poor in spirit. We've been granted the gift to receive and to give love in the most dramatic way.

> "But love your enemies and do good to them" (Luke 6:35). To destroy our enemies requires an army. To love them requires community.
>
> "Let your love be genuine. Hate what is evil" (Romans 12:9). A white-hot genuine love is stoked in the fires of white-hot believers gathered together. When we're alone, we often tolerate what should be hated.

But in community we take what breaks the heart of God and put it on the ash heap where it belongs.

"Love your neighbor as yourself" (Mark 12:31). We are prone to ignore our neighbors. But community propels us to acknowledge them and invite them alongside of us. At some point we must acknowledge and act on the fact that Jesus is calling us to love those who are literally our neighbors.

"Love is patient, love is kind. It does not envy, it does not boast, it is not proud. It does not dishonor others, it is not self-seeking, it is not easily angered, it keeps no record of wrongs. Love does not delight in evil but rejoices with the truth. It always protects, always trusts, always hopes, always perseveres" (1 Corinthians 13:4–7). Patience, kindness, humility, honor, forgiveness, and praise all flow from love. These verses have been relegated to wedding ceremonies, but they should be our war cries as we put our flesh and our desires to death.

"There is no fear in love. But perfect love casts out fear" (1 John 4:18). Fear is tolerated in isolation. It's cultivated in private. But in community, faith is the trump card. Anxiety, worry, and angst are commonplace, even expected in the world. But in community, we cast out the darkness of fear with the light of love.

"Greater love has no one than this: to lay down one's life for one's friends" (John 15:13). Around the table we aren't asking, How are you doing? Not that we are unconcerned. But the more pressing question is, How are you dying? We are less concerned with how people are grabbing hold of their dreams and more concerned with how they are laying down their lives. This is no short order. Many will push away from the table at this command, at this expectation. But at the table of community, this is what we are after—a greater love.

APPLICATION

I don't know of a more practical exercise of faith than sitting around the table with others. The tangible nature of eating and listening makes us believe (and rightly so!) that something important is happening. It reminds us that there is nowhere to go but to the people sitting across from us. Somehow casseroles become sacred in this marriage of friends. Wine and coffee, these unlikely sacraments, can remind us of our humanness. Conversation and chemistry and children in the background all signify to us that this is what life looks like when it's done on purpose. No road map, but we know where we are headed. Meals bind us together. Ideas, like flavors, blend into a single profile. This is what happens when we do the work of staying and giving and praying and learning together around this meal. It would certainly be easier to keep the doors locked and reheat leftovers than to do what we've suggested. Easier, but not better. This application section is going to require more of you. Sowing and reaping. Sowing and reaping. Plant well in this next season and you can have faith that something good will spring up when you need it most.

1. Invite a few friends over to simply talk about God's language in your life. Pass out pieces of paper with words like grace, provision, hope, forgiveness, and redemption and ask each person to share a story around each word.
2. Do a topical bible study on the subject of meals. Record how many times Jesus does ministry around food.
3. Do a little digging—investigate someone in your circle of friends who has a real financial need and find a way to meet that need.
4. Write ten personal notes, encouraging people for their compassion and generosity.
5. Make a meal and take it to a neighbor you don't really know. Just because.
6. Pray for someone. As in, an out-loud, in the moment, prayer for a friend in need.

5

The Living Room is for Longevity

THE LIVING ROOM IS the place where we live. This isn't word play. Just as the dining room is the place where we dine, the living room is the place where we live. And yet if someone asks us, "What happens in this room?" We'd most likely cock our heads sideways and say, "Well, this room is like the relational junk drawer of the house. Whatever we don't do in the kitchen, foyer, bedroom, or bathroom gets dumped in the living room."

At least, that's how this room works in my house. The living room tends to be the place without a lot of purpose or intention. We kick back and relax here. We Netflix, take naps, and curl up with a good book here.

A helpful question might be, What kind of actual living is happening in this room? In particular, how is gospel-driven, loneliness-extinguishing, joy-inducing, incarnate living and breathing happening in this place?

Truth be told, the living room feels like the place we wait around in until something of substance happens. We relent to perceived reality and assume that there are some unredeemable, unspiritual things we do as humans. Not evil per se, but the parts of our lives that are in the background . . . in the margin. Waiting in lines. Sitting at traffic lights. Mowing the grass. Getting the oil changed. These activities all feel unredeemable. Not wicked or broken, but the in-between of real living. And yet such a huge portion of our lives are lived in those places. In the middle. In the margin. In the gray areas that don't seem to carry much influence—conversations that orbit around the cost of diapers or the recent broken arm or the plight of SEC football. We're told by the spiritual experts that these conversations are inconsequential. Meaningless even. Move past them quickly, we're told. Engage in something important.

We begin to wonder if these are the conversations the Apostle Paul was talking about when he warned Timothy, "Avoid godless chatter" (2 Timothy 2:16). We're convinced our time could be better spent talking about global warming or the plight of battered seals or the sex trade. But I don't think that's what Paul had in mind.

Surely, he understood that much of life is lived in the in-between. Somewhere in the middle of carting the kids to little league or picking up pizzas after a long day at work. Life is happening all around us. Mostly, it feels like life is happening to us. It's not the fullness of life, not the John 10:10 sort of life that is quixotically promised from the pulpit. It's certainly not the life we dream of, but it's the real thing nonetheless.

Theologians have a fancy name for this in between area of life—inaugurated eschatology. The-now-and-not-yet of living. That is, life will come to a glorious end one day and all things will be made right, but until then ... we're stuck in the middle. The waiting period.

I'd like to suggest that the waiting, the middle part of living, doesn't have to be wasted. It's the part of life that will never get scrapbooked or filed away as important, but it will most certainly be the portion that is likely to shape us most. Do you know why? Because most of our time is spent here.

Our relationships are filled with millions of mundane, yet sacred moments. And it's those sacrosanct ticks of the clock where our relationships go deep. The arc of our relationships is bent toward the regular monotony of life. That's not a bad thing. Vanilla living is what most of us have. We'd all love to be the Rocky Road or the Tooty Fruity of life experience, but we still have to go to work, pay the bills, and work out our salvation with fear and trembling (Philippians 2:12). Most of life doesn't feel big. But the overwhelming contribution of small moments will inevitably take us to deep and sometimes big places.

WE ARE NOT PROFESSIONALS

Pastoral care is a phrase that is used regularly in my vocation. If you were an IT specialist you'd probably talk about bandwidth. A mechanic might mention torque wrenches and brake jobs. In my line of work, it's pastoral care. It's a churchy way to say that we take care of people's hearts. People like me, you know, the church professional types, think we've got the market cornered on pastoral care. After all, we're ordained and have advanced degrees and can parse a Greek word. Any dope knows I have been given heavenly authority to care for people in the most spiritual way possible.

That's ridiculous, of course. When I start believing I'm the most qualified person in the room or the most acutely aware of how to pastor people, I refer back to a book that shaped my early days as a pastor: *Brothers, We Are* Not *Professionals*. The title says it all. The ordained, the organized and highly educated usually have no idea what to do in the mess and mass of real human need. If you want me to give a sermon, I'm your man. But pastoral care? I'm still learning. I fake it much of the time. I plaster on a smile, recite my practiced, medicinal liturgy about God's plan or his mercy over a broken life. And it's not that my liturgy isn't true. It's more than true. God's plan and His mercy carry heavenly and human weight when people lose their bearings. But just speaking these words over someone's clinical depression or recent divorce is like pasting a band aid on someone with stage 4 cancer. They need more than words, more than a professional.

We pastoral types seem to think Sunday morning is the best time to shepherd hearts and speak into deeply personal situations. In our defense, everyone is already in one place, lined up in rows. Everyone is cleaned up and ready to receive help from God. The mistake, however, is thinking that the guy on stage with the face mic is the best person available. Not to say we don't receive from corporate teaching and instruction. Not to say there isn't supreme benefit in singing our songs together as a singular tribe. I'm not beginning to suggest some version of pastoral care can't happen in a large gathering. It can. It's just not normative to shepherd a heart with hundreds of other people present. What I'd like to contend is that the point of pastors, the professional types, isn't just to pastor. Our job is to help others learn to pastor, to care for the souls around them. Some call it the Cure of Souls (Latin: cura animarum). A more modern meaning would be the care of souls.

"And he gave the apostles, the prophets, the evangelists, the shepherds and teachers, to equip the saints for the work of ministry, for building up the body of Christ..." (Ephesians 4:11–12). Who are the saints? We are. You are. The ones without an office or ordination certificate doing the work of ministry. The advice to this young church— don't leave this supremely important thing of soul care to the "professionals" —is at the center of communal living.

The Living Room is for Longevity

Curing or caring or loving is for those who walk alongside. This means you have what it takes to do the supreme work of shepherding hearts.

It's in the middle, the in-between—the living room of life—where most of this pastoral care takes place. You might be wondering, what does this look like? What does pastoral care mean? What does a shepherd do? She protects. He feeds. She cares for. We give tough love, tender love, needed guidance, heartful correction.

A shepherd in the ancient world was someone who lived with the sheep. Knew each by name. Had an eye on the rebel and a shepherd's crook close to the frail. Shepherds in ancient culture were at the bottom of the social ladder. They were the rejected and dirty. Shepherds were the opposite of professional. It's a beautiful reminder that those who were first to hear the good news of great joy coming into the world were shepherds in the field, not professionals in the city. So it seems that in God's economy, shepherds rank high in the kingdom of heaven. That's you and me—the shepherds.

But specifically, what are we shepherding? Transitions mostly. With each stage of life comes new (or very old) challenges to face. We need to be careful not to minimize the power of a painful transition to ruin a life. When a single man or woman moves into marriage, we shepherd them in this transition. We gently ask how life has changed now that there is another person in the house. What has it been like for them not to get their way 100% of the time? Are they learning to forgive and communicate and argue in a way that truly honors the other person as an image bearer of God?

This may seem intrusive to you at first glance. But in every other area of life there are people there to help us transition into new seasons. Doctors are the first who help us transition from our mother's womb to the outside world. Teachers help us transition from one grade or one school to another. If you think about it, we all carry this joyful burden to help people move beyond where they are to where they should be. Transitions abound and that is where most of pastoral care takes place.

As our little tribe gathers weekly at my home, we have to be careful not to be spiritual policeman regulating people's behavior. We're not out to systematize our relationships. We're simply working at living well. In addition, we don't want to be parental figures in which we give nods of approval or disapproval to life choices. And we're not just friends who gather on couches sharing life experiences without any real access to personal feedback. No, we're shepherds.

There is a gospel weight to the role we play in each other's lives. When we see someone in our little community goading us for personal approval, we stop and probe his heart. What's going on? What is feeding this insecurity? If a person seems to be posturing or bragging or making the gathering about her, we gently correct and encourage her to be "quick to listen and slow to speak" (James 1:19). When someone shows up hurting, we stop what we're doing and pray—for them, with them. This isn't an event to get through. This is shepherding in the moment.

Mostly, we're teaching each other how to live together in the middle places. And boy, do we need help. From the moment we start breathing air, we enter into an education of upward mobility, adapting, making a mark on the world. We are taught very early how to live in public spaces. Fit in, get along, avoid conflict, be successful, smile. While you and I have mastered the art of living a public persona (usually, a fraudulent one), we have yet to be comfortable in our own skin when no one is watching. This is where we need the most support. The most shepherding.

SMALL LIFE

I like theology. I read it, study it, preach it. It's the framework for my vocation. But most people just assume that I like to talk theology all the time. It gets awkward. I'll bump into a friend at Wal-Mart and inevitably the conversation will get steered to the bible or the resurrection or church. I stumble at first, feeling out of place, disoriented by crying children in shopping carts, all the while thinking that I don't really know what Exodus 14 or substitutionary atonement has to do with my armful of toilet paper. I mumble something spiritually appropriate and escape to the next aisle. It's usually after encounters like this that I realize that most people are terrible at small talk. They don't know what to say, so they go big. In fact, even the name "small talk" implies that it has no real place at the adult table. I think we have this terribly wrong. Small talk may lead us to big talk, but what's wrong with small talk in the first place? The humdrum is where life is lived and that's where we want to be—where people live. If we are constantly pushing people up the mountain because that's where we convince them God lives, no one will be content to live ordinary, faithful lives in the plains.

If we are only present in the big moments of others' lives and not in the small moments, we misunderstand our capacity for real love. We would turn into the weekend parent who only shows up for Chuck E Cheese and

The Living Room is for Longevity

the amusement park but has no idea what is really happening in the day to day of his child's life. The admission price for the memories we hold dear is paid in very unmemorable car rides and weekly coffee dates. Because we find that those moments, mundane as they are, actually matter.

The "unimportant" parts of ministry, the things that we do when we don't think we are doing anything significant, might make the most difference. There is no such thing as small talk. What exists is talk. And it was by talk, words from God, that the world was created. There is no small power in very normal words. We like to think there is such a thing as big talk or small talk. We wonder if there is a communion with friends that is more sacred than another. I don't think so. This isn't to say there aren't moments in which a conversation carries a weight and urgency and delight in the Lord more than others. Those conversations are typically ordained and scheduled by God himself. But every other conversation about house paint and horseplay is still sacred. There are no wasted words among those with whom we walk.

Small moments matter too. My wife has been intentional to build these seemingly unimportant moments with our kids into our schedule. Thursday night is game night. We order pizza and pull out any number of board games. Our kids love it. Nothing special happens. Just routine. Every week we eat and roll dice. And every week I lose. The conversation never goes more than an inch deep. High fives and laughter usually abound. No bibles are present. We don't pray and ask God to give us good attitudes when we lose (though I probably should pray that.) I don't sermonize the evils of real-life Monopoly. We are simply enjoying each other.

I'm sure our kids will remember the trips to Disney World, but their best memories will be those that were part of our household rhythm. They will look back and think, "I don't remember many of the details of game night, but I do remember we were together every week." That's what we're after with others in the small moments of life.

I think it's tragic that we plan and save for the big moments of life (weddings, babies, and retirement) but we miss the beauty and weight of all of the small, daily, insignificant moments. We invest our life savings and best energy in the few big boulders of life, but in reality, our best and most consistent time is given to the small, sacred seconds of life.

Is it possible that we have mixed up our priorities? That we have put too much emphasis on the big and overlooked the small?

The Old Testament prophet Malachi understood this when he penned these words, "Then those who feared the Lord talked with each other, and the Lord listened and heard. A scroll of remembrance was written in his presence concerning those who feared the Lord and honored his name" (Malachi 3:16). When the people of God simply sit and talk, interjecting the faithfulness of God in the routine and rhythm of life, it catches the attention of God. We spend so much time asking God to do big things, never taking note of the millions of little things he does without us even asking. So he tells this remnant people, "I'm not only interested in the whopping, sea splitting moments. Yes, I will do those. But pay attention to the tiny, easy to miss seconds of grace. If you'll search me out there, I'll take note and heaven will open up for you right there in the midst of the mundane."

We must recapture the small moments and small conversations that make up our lives. Because if our scrapbooks are only filled with the places we've been, but not of the people who have gotten us there, then we've misunderstood every small moment given to us by God. What brings merit to these times is seeing the sojourners alongside of us as infinitely valuable. Just being with them counts for something in heaven.

How does this work?

The problem with small moments is that they are often demonized in our culture. "Do something big! Don't live a small life!" we are told. During every visit to the movie theater and in every reprise of a commercial, we hear cheering for those who color outside the lines, who do more than just the status quo. The heroes of our world are those who live fast, die young, and are impatient enough to make life happen on their own terms. We deify these people. Small living is rejected as if it's merely small thinking.

However, the Apostle Paul tells us, "Make it your ambition to lead a quiet life . . ." (2 Thessalonians 4:11). A quiet life is a life of beautiful, often uncelebrated faithfulness. The end of the day comes and we have to think back to what we did. But we can take heart and know that the small conversations about nothing in particular, with people of importance, somehow fill the big holes in our hearts. Small living is not small thinking. Rather, it's the ability to see each moment as a gift that makes life beautiful and expectant. Coffee with friends, leftovers with neighbors, running errands with a buddy from community group—all these are fantastically ordinary flashes to be treasured. We don't begrudge them. We hold on to them. These are the in-between moments, and they matter.

BIG PEOPLE

Microscopes make small things appear bigger. Telescopes make things that seem small, because they're seen at a distance, appear as they really are . . . big.[1] When we begin to live with people in the in-between of life, we begin to see people as they really are. Perhaps they had previously appeared small, when seen from a distance. But now that they're brought near, we see them as they really are . . . big. Not larger than life. But important. Valuable. Quirky. Fascinating. Unique. Dream-filled people.

Our culture is in the microscope business. Our best time and energy are given to make small lives appear big. We over-inflate, posture our accomplishments, and tweet every good deed for the world to see. We want to be perceived as big. In doing so, we champion all the wrong ideas because we are looking in the microscope of the world rather than the telescope of God. We confuse talent with maturity, gifting with character, money with security, and shouting with authority. Microscope living.

The in-between of life is filled with people, and when we look at these people through the lens of God, we see them as they really are. Not necessarily big people, but people who are now visible to us. We see them now. When we spend considerable time with these men and women, we are able to look past their perceived economic value to us. That is, rather than seeing them for what they can give to us, what value they can offer to our lives, we begin to see them as innately prized, just as they are. No longer are they seen as a business contact or a prospect. These are real people who are fundamentally precious, not because of what they contribute, but because of who they are.

People matter. All people.

Ironically, it's often in the small moments when we identify the big people. The Tuesday afternoon coffee with a friend; the Saturday morning garage sale with a few ladies you hold dear; the football game with an old friend. It's in the small moments that the veil is ripped away and your eyes clearly see who is walking alongside you—big people.

I am certainly not discounting the big moments in life when important people show up. We might consider them big people too. The friend who sits with you in crisis. The mom who coaches you in labor. The college roommate who consoles you after the divorce. These are critical moments in life when

---

1. John Piper, A Peculiar Glory, (Wheaton, Crossway, 2016), 203

God brings just the right person to guide you back from the edge. These are often people who play a significant, trajectory-altering role in your story.

But we also can't overlook the people we argue with, cry with, binge watch with, and babysit with. They are the ones who live with us in the in-between. We don't necessarily see them as significant, but their presence has kept us on the rails throughout this God journey. These are the people who God brings into our lives to settle in. Who are present before and after the crisis. They are stay-ers. They linger after the smoke has cleared. I contend that they are the biggest people in our stories. They actually know you. They know your frailties and have seen you at your worst, and yet they keep showing up. They probably have the extra key to your house and know where you keep the secret stash of chocolate or wine (or both). They know you don't really have your act together. It has been years since you've picked up the living room or kitchen before they came by. They don't ask about opening the fridge or pouring a cup of coffee. They just do it. They belong in your life. They know you, and more importantly, they love you in the in-between times. This is a very difficult place to get to in a relationship—to be fully known and to still be fully loved.

A Choice

When we get to this place in community, we typically behave in one of three ways. We get nervous and begin to hold back; we end the friendship; or we go all in. Because we are a guarded people, holding back and ending the friendship is what makes the most economic sense. We don't want to lose too much, we think. We've spent all we can afford. And if it starts getting too real and too raw, we tend to press the reset button on the relationship. We are desperately afraid it will be found out that we are perpetually broken. And yet when we take the chance to fully reveal who we are, where we've been, where our faith has failed, and find that we are still loved, a shift takes place—we discover that this is a person who is important. A big person. This is when we learn to hold on to these people because they have been holding on to us.

These regular people, who happen to be present in the insignificant times of life, remind us that crisis is not the norm. Some people are made for crisis. Battle-scarred, war-torn, adrenalin junkies. They are never fully alive unless everything is at stake. We need those people when life falls apart. They help us navigate perilous decisions when our minds are not clear. However, life in the in-between is filled with very little crisis. Calm waters abound. Quiet. Even boring days at times. These people we've begun to walk deeply with remind us that life is just as important when unimportant things are happening. We become tethered to peaceful and sacred living when we do this over the longterm. Otherwise, we just feel like we're licking our wounds from one conflict, blowup, and meltdown to another. Crisis becomes our normal. Truly important people, regular people, keep us anchored to the everyday and remind us of how sacred times of nothing-in-particular actually are.

Joe and Patty were that to us. The past-tense of that last sentence hurts me even now. We felt their absence most acutely in the middle part of our lives. In the mundane. But eventually, Amy and I found that we had licked our wounds long enough and we were back doing the work of cultivating new friendships and opening our house to a fresh community. We had invited a few people into the middle space of our lives. It takes time though. The middle place is hard to get to. And middle place people are even harder to find. Intertwined routines and late-night conversations about nothing in particular are cultivated only after the journey through the foyer and kitchen. Frankly, we had no idea something so mundane could give us so much life. We learned (and only later appreciated) that normal is living in quiet rhythm with others who seek the same thing.

It seems this is what Jesus had with his friends too. I say it seems that way because the New Testament is primarily the highlights—the stories and sermons of renown. Even John the apostle says, "Now there are also many other things that Jesus did. Were every one of them to be written, I suppose that the world itself could not contain the books that would be written" (John 21:25). I imagine lots of in-between time with Jesus and the disciples. Times of walking and eating and laughing. I don't think every word that came out of Jesus' mouth had eternal significance. And yet just being with him in the in-between is what bound these men together.

REST IN THE MIDDLE

For three years straight, right after church, I watched the movie *Shawshank Redemption*. If you haven't seen the film, put this book down right now and go watch it. You will be a better person for it. Shawshank became a sort of two-hour therapy session for me. I needed to be reminded every Sunday that redemption is possible. I needed to be assured that no matter how bad a situation gets, something better is coming. The gospel of Jesus communicates this with astounding clarity and passion. But I forget. So

God in his relentless patience uses other mediums to remind me—nature, music, old books, and Shawshank.

Week after week, while planting a brand new church and feeling the weight of this new family's life or death on my shoulders, I needed a break. I needed a predictable, inconsequential lift of encouragement. I needed rest. And rest happens in this place of in-between. It can't happen in any other place. For those who are not seeking safe spaces and sacred relationships in the in-between, weariness can be downright deadly. Exhaustion naturally arcs towards isolation. Language like, "I just need to work this out on my own," or "I need some me time" creep in, and the recovery that is so desperately sought is never really found. Do you know why? Recovery, at least sustainable recovery, cannot happen alone. We need each other, even in the downtime.

"Therefore, since the promise of entering his rest still stands, let us be careful that none of you be found to have fallen short of it. For we also have had the good news proclaimed to us, just as they did; but the message they heard was of no value to them, because they did not share the faith of those who obeyed. Now we who have believed enter that rest . . ." (Hebrews 4:1–3). The author of Hebrews understood that rest is always available, but it's rarely enjoyed alone. Many of us believe rest is found with our doors closed and our lives on lockdown. This is why rest in community is so critical, but rarely discovered.

Unfortunately, it's in this middle part of life where we make the worst decisions. When lives becomes eerily quiet we become suspicious that something is wrong. Mid-life crises are third-cousins to this in-between weariness. Our lethargy turns into inertia, which breeds depression, that leads to poor decisions, which then torpedoes us into inaccessibility. I call it the cycle of exhaustion. The only cure is real rest.

Rest isn't simply the absence of activity. Rest is a person. Jesus is the only one who can give us sustainable respite in the deep places. He is the only one in whom the burden of performance and the pride of success gets muted. I'm not talking about a vacation, but a true reprieve from the pressure of being someone or doing something or producing one more widget that turns a head.

I am embarrassed by how often I respond to a general, "How are you?" with a hurried, "I'm busy." I don't even realize I'm saying it. It's the default setting on my mouth. Sadly, my response tells the inquisitor two things: Firstly, I am out of control. My calendar is ruling me. Others around me dictate my time. And because of their priority I have no time for the one standing in front of me. Secondly, I am proclaiming with unwavering confidence, I am important!

It's ironic that I dismiss people in this way since I'm in a people-centric vocation. But like the world, my busyness has become a badge of honor. It becomes the thing that guides my heart and determines my worth.

Theologically, busyness is born out of self-importance and nurtured by false worship. Our busyness is birthed from the belief that we are needed, important, and critical to life's events. And while intrinsically we are valuable, we are not inherently needed. I know that's a bummer, but quit your job tomorrow and see what I mean. Your company will keep on moving without you. Your office will have someone else's nameplate on the door by next Tuesday. They love you, but they don't really need you.

And yet the lie of self-importance keeps us striving. We believe that getting what we deserve, what we have worked for, takes preeminence over God's promise that he will be our daily bread (Exodus 16:4). Our busyness in every spare moment is our idolatrous confession that God will not provide for us and the burden for provision is ultimately on our shoulders.

A recent survey revealed that the average person checks a text, email, or social media on a device every six minutes.[2] Think about that. Every six minutes we invite a thousand virtual opinions into our already overcrowded soul. Opinions regarding who we should be, what we should wear, and what we should be doing. We are either starved for information or desperate for affirmation. Either way, our busyness reaffirms the lie that life is about us.

"Therefore, since the promise of entering his rest still stands, let us be careful that none of you be found to have fallen short of it. For we also have had the good news proclaimed to us, just as they did; but the message they heard was of no value to them because they did not share the faith of those who obeyed. Now we who have believed enter that rest..." (Hebrews 4:1–3).

The writer of Hebrews gives us a sober warning. Rest is possible, but it is not natural. Rest is plausible, but never on our own terms.

"Let us be careful . . . For we also . . . Just as they . . . Now we who have believed enter that rest . . ." In the first three verses about entering rest, the writer uses ten pronouns that imply togetherness. We. Us. They. The author is building a case: biblical rest is only possible in deep community.

---

2. Ben Parr, "Social Networking Accounts for 1 of Every 6 Minutes Spent Online," Mashable, Last Modified June 15, 2011, Accessed June 2, 2018, https://mashable.com/2011/06/15/social-networking-accounts-for-1-of-every-6-minutes-spent-online-stats/#3iACAK9uy5qz

The Hebrew writer says we will "fall short" of real rest if we pursue it in isolation. We may take the needed vacation, but we don't ever feel the soul rest we know we need. What we first need is the we.

Put this in terms of a great symphony. One hundred instruments creating enormous movement and then a repose—a flutter of sound and then a break. Glorious noise and then nothing. The musical term for the period of time when there is no music, no sound, no movement is rest. One of the things that makes the symphony so striking is that the great cloud of violins and cellos and trumpets all know the exact time to stop playing. The rest. A communal rest. All at once, on purpose. In fact, it is only in the rest that we can appreciate the movement. We see this in the creation account as well. The Trinity—God in community—speaks the world into existence. Earth from heaven. Light from darkness. Land from sea. Man from dust. Six days God labors. And then . . . he rests. He gives this example to man and then includes a command, "Keep the Sabbath day holy" (Exodus 20:8). Work and rest. Work and rest. Work and rest. This is the great rhythm that God has prepared for us, even in community.

When we walk with others in the in-between, we are able to see where the fractures are. Like a cracked pot put up to the light, an unhurried, attentive, and even slow pastoral approach helps us to see with clarity where the broken places are. All at once we are able to see with a gospel clarity. It's in these times that we whisper to those we're walking with, "Slow down. Put away the phone. Stop answering emails. Be present. Be at rest."

When we are walking in the kind of community that is given permission to speak the hard truth of rest into our lives, we know we have found treasure. It's in these deep waters where those who love us can remind you and me that we are not as important as we think we are.

Rest is found when we lay down the belief that we are not God's gift to life. Deep, gospel friends are brave enough to remind us that our busyness is not a virtue to boast in, but rather, a sin to be confessed. Rest is experienced when those we are doing life with gently help us disconnect from the unrealistic expectations of a furiously busy world.

Busyness is a form of idolatry because it is misplaced worship. Our best energy and attentions are given as fragrant offerings at the altar of the American dream. This kind of worship causes us to believe that if we go and go and go, then one day we will be rewarded with the iconic rest—e.g., retirement, vacations, etc.—that we have been promised. But ultimately, busyness is only a treadmill. We run and run and run, but we never actually go anywhere that matters.

Like all the other broken cisterns of our culture (see Jeremiah 2:13), busyness will never satisfy the deep desire of our hearts to be fulfilled, loved, and accepted. This idolatry of busyness is perhaps one of the most dangerous because it is often celebrated as a quality to be admired, when it's really just a tool of the enemy that leads us further from the heart of God.

The only escape from idolatry comes when we smash those little gods. Take the statues of pride, self-importance, insecurity, and fear of failure and grind them into dust. Healthy community will help you gather up these modern Baals and guarantee their demise. Our rest is a matter of life and death and is dependent on others who walk with us in the middle.

APPLICATION

I have a weird compulsion about my living room. Before Amy and I sit down to watch television, I make sure the living room is cleaned up, vacuumed and tidy. This is certainly a poor reflection on my broken soul and my need for control. However, the good news is that I know this little impulse doesn't work in real life. The living room of life is designed to be a little messy. Cause, you know, people are in it. This application section is designed to be disruptive to your schedule of clean lines and busy life.

1. Make a list of ten people who have been involved in your life for ten years or more. Write each one of them an email thanking them for simply being present in the important and unimportant times.

2. Invite your neighbors over to watch a movie this weekend. That's it.

3. Catalog five mundane conversations you had from the previous week. Then spend a few minutes praying for each of those people that God put in your path.

4. Limit your TV time to no more than one hour per day for the next week. Press into the silence of your home. Journal your thoughts about why it is hard to be alone and what God is trying to accomplish in your heart.

5. Invite two families (or four singles) to a weekend of sabbath rest. Rent a cabin, go camping, etc . . . Ask each person to read and meditate on the same bible passages. At the end of each night come back together to discuss how God has been using the time.

6

The Garage is for Growing Up

WHEN AMY AND I were shopping for our first home, we were in over our heads. It turns out that the real estate world is complicated. We had no idea about the insider language that was meant to keep outsiders in the dark. We loved to read through the house listings inserted in the Sunday newspaper. "Quaint and modest starter home." Holy cow! That was what we needed. In our excitement we made an appointment with a realtor. It turns out that quaint and modest was code for "shoebox residence built for Hobbits." An ad read, "Rustic, romantic feel. Perfect for the housing pioneer." We were quickly learning to read between the lines. Translation? "Expensive fixer-upper with old plumbing." The promise of "an amazing location and great views. Interior needs some TLC," would be more aptly described as "Cul de sac home. Triple homicide. Clean-up required." Before we ever paid a cent toward a mortgage we were already exhausted by the process.

When we walked into what turned out to be our dream home on 5th Avenue East, we had no idea what to expect. What we found was that the hardwood floors were beautiful and the kitchen had been updated. There was a great front porch and a window seat in the bedroom. 900 square feet of love is what we said. We made an offer that afternoon and moved in a month later. Within the first 24 hours of being homeowners, we realized we might have overlooked a few critical items. For example, the garage. That is, there wasn't one. I thought, how had we missed something so obvious? I was not happy.

To be fair, the garage is the least praised part of a home. We never parade friends through the two-car storage area littered with boxes and oil stains. We never post photos of how we rearranged the stacked boxes in the corner of this space. We take the garage for granted. And usually the best way to discover we have taken something for granted is to have it removed.

I've never felt more in need in home ownership than when I didn't have this space. Where will we store things? Park things, hang things, hide things? Mostly, where will we repair things?

This is certainly true in this house of community. We create, enjoy, and cultivate in the living quarters. But when things go wrong, we confess, correct, and rehab in the garage. Unfortunately, the foyer is where most people live, comfortable with the coming and going of relative strangers. Few enter the kitchen of discovery. Fewer still make it around a table. But the garage? Only the brave. Those filled with faith venture here. Those who know that God's painful grace is always helpful. Too often, we either build a house without a garage, thinking the hard work of heart repair will be done by the professionals, or our garages end up being ordered and clean, but rarely used.

CLEAN GARAGES MEAN EMPTY HOUSES

Most Saturdays in the spring and summer I was forced to wave to Joe as he mowed his yard. Seeing Patty planting flowers alongside her husband only added to the relational awkwardness. We smiled and ached our way through years of hurt. We endured several years of relative quiet. Somewhere around year three, the four of us found our way around a table at Starbucks. Talk of forgiveness and redemption was sprinkled through the conversation. I was still hurting though. I couldn't do it. Not because they carried the weight of blame. Not even close. I just couldn't find a way through it.

But by year four, my hurt and pain had cooled. Amy and Patty had run into each other at the farmer's market and subsequently met for coffee. They decided to get the four of us together for dinner. I was assured that it really was just dinner. No heavy talk, I demanded. Chicken casserole and a bottle of wine and lots of awkward silence is what ensued. I was nervous thinking a bomb was about to go off. Then I remembered that the bomb had already detonated four years earlier. These little dinner dates happened three or four more times over the course of the spring. One night the conversation turned serious. It turned to the Hiroshima that was our friendship and how our little community surrounding it had died. Tears all around. By this time, they were tears of regret and pain, not tears of anger.

Over the course of the next few weeks we gathered together with greater intentionality and we found ourselves in repair mode. Reconciliation was happening. Slowly. We had stepped into the garage of community and were doing the impossible work of grace.

Those who have chosen a life of community know that things will break—and it's usually hearts that break. Expectations too. The pain of relational loss is something to be anticipated in this kind of venture. More than that, we quickly discover that relationships require constant care. Otherwise, friendships fracture, conflict occurs, and communication wanes. The garage of community calls us to become practitioners—relational mechanics and plumbers and electricians walking deeply with a few others, keenly aware of the challenges, but unafraid of the work required. Otherwise, we continue to trade in the cracked and broken friendships that need some TLC for the shiny, new ones that inevitably keep us chained to surface-level, foyer living. Our failure to persevere in community, doing the hard work of repairing broken relationships, causes us to perpetually start over.

In the garage, we get our hands dirty and invite others to do the same. We're not playing in the dirt here. We're doing spiritual work that creates necessary callouses because we're holding on hard to something that really matters. Ultimately, the garage is the place where freedom is born. In my imagination I can see an unfinished wooden plaque hanging in the Apostle Paul's garage that reads, "For freedom's sake." Paul knew that freedom could only come at a cost. Not just the unimaginable cost of the Son of God, but the cost of our own lives as well.

"It is for freedom that Christ has set us free" (Galatians 5:1, NIV). Paul is a wordsmith. A prophet and a poet too. Follow this gospel gem in reverse. ". . .you were set free." That is, you are free because of Jesus. Free from your past, the guilt of your sin, the shame of your darkest moments, and the humiliation of a tortured eternity. You were set free through the work of Christ. The reason? For freedom. Meaning, your freedom is for your freedom's sake. For those who trust Jesus, a freedom moment occurs—salvation. Sonship. Daughtership. Forgiveness. Your name is heard around the throne in heaven. A moment is all God needs to change the trajectory of our lives.

However, Paul seems to be saying that a freedom moment begets more freedom moments—for freedom you were set free. The taste of grace hooks us like an addict. Our souls long for a greater amount of what we already possess—freedom. When we experience this gift of grace, we never want to go back to bondage, which is what the world calls normal.

Bondage is not reserved only for the past. It can trap a person in the present as well. It can anchor someone to an idea or attitude or behavior that appears normal in some circles, but under the bright light of gospel community, it is seen to be broken. This isn't necessarily about sin; though sin is destructive enough. A person's bondage often has less to do with the forgiveness of God over his life, and more to do with the feeling of worthlessness and broken identity attached to his sin. That is, shame is the little voice in our heads that convinces us that our worst moments define us. That kind of bondage keeps us disconnected from experiencing the newness of life that we know is available. We end up believing we are forgiven, but not ever fully free from our sin.

Francis had been part of our community for about a year. She was tender, kind, and acutely aware of others' needs. Francis was the kind of person everyone wants as a friend. It wasn't unusual for her to text or call regularly to let us know she was praying for us. She was generous with her time and she regularly sought out ways to affirm others around her. Francis was the prototype of what we were looking for in deep community. Over time though, I noticed things were a little too clean. Too ordered. Her Christian language was too rehearsed. Too on-time. I don't know if that makes sense to you. But I find that the longer a person lives in the church world, but not in deep relationship, accurate spiritual language is spoken, but the heart is usually neglected. This was Francis. I want to make sure you're seeing this picture accurately. Francis was giving and praying and loving and leading, but she never actually shared anything about herself. We knew that she was from Ohio, that she liked to ski, that she had a toddler. But most of what we knew was generic information we could learn by checking the census bureau. We wanted to know more, we wanted to really know who Francis was. Eventually we asked her why she was behaving like someone in witness protection. She quickly deflected with a perfectly timed bible verse about being interested in others , about counting others more important than yourself (Philippians 2:3). We assured Francis that we understood the value of humility, but what we really wanted was to walk with her in deep places. Like many others, Francis was convinced that the best way to get over her past was to bury it. After much assurance of our love and support, Francis tentatively opened up to our community. It turns out that Francis hadn't always been as "put together" as we had believed. What we saw was a business executive with a loving husband and a young child. But Francis had a dark history that left a soul full of scars. Buried beneath years of shame and guilt, Francis was terrified of being found out. Sharing her story of drug abuse and sex addiction, years of one-night stands and a decade of sexual confusion, had opened up a dam of pain.

In that moment, our living room was transformed into a garage. We prayed. We cried. We walked with her through her confession, helping to bring her past into the present so that God could deal with it. Redemption and healing flooded our little space. We watched God begin to restore, putting someone back together right in front of our eyes. God graciously allowed us to be gospel mechanics, getting our hands dirty as we ministered to Francis. Most of us were exhausted by the end of our time. We witnessed something vast and broad and glorious—like standing at the west rim of the Grand Canyon. But instead, in my little suburban home, there weren't words to describe seeing someone emerge from a dark place of shame. It was for freedom that Francis was set free!

During seasons in which our little community is doing the hard work of heart repair, I hold tightly onto 1 Corinthians 15:10— "But by the grace of God I am what I am, and his grace toward me was not in vain. On the contrary, I worked harder than any of them, though it was not I, but the grace of God that is with me." It is the sweet reminder of two things for me: Grace is at work—in me and around me. My frailties do not put a halt to God's supernatural work in this space. I need this reminder because more times than not (usually in the middle space of living), it doesn't feel like God is doing anything in particular. But he is. He is always at work. "My Father is working until now, and I am working" (John 5:17). Secondly, I'm reminded that this thing of community is hard. This is not a revelation. Community is soul-wearying, even on good days. Friendship is hard. It requires the best from us. I remind myself that it is fully normative to be tired and often fatigued in this work of reconciliation. Joy is still present. This is how I know we are doing something that matters.

If the work of freedom is the hallmark of the garage, then the tools we use as we pursue freedom should be well worn. In the context of community, each of us should not only have the experience of personal emancipation from the shame of our past, but also plenty of experience with setting others free.

PROPHETIC LISTENING

One of the basic tools we need as we work for freedom is the tool of listening. Listening is like a hammer or screwdriver—it's a tool that must be in the toolbox of anyone intent on walking deeply with others. This tool requires no formal education or insight into the psyche. It can be used by anyone who is willing and able to still the mind and heart. We are not talking about the typical practice of distracted listening that we employ in our day to day lives. What we need is what therapists might call active listening. Priests and pastors would call it counseling. New Testament mystics might call it the prophetic voice.

This kind of listening is the ability to attune our ears to the person in front of us— actively engaged in his story, hurt, scars, and pain—while simultaneously attuning our ear to Jesus and what he is saying. This kind of listening is akin to how a good diagnostic physician listens to your family history and description of your problems, while simultaneously making connections between what you report and what he knows from experience and avid study. The things he hears from you, paired with the things he knows and the things he sees during his thorough examination, work together to formulate a reliable and accurate diagnosis. In community, we too are called to listen attentively, like a physician intent on seeing what is real.

This tool appears passive. But it is intensely active, because God is involved. Once God has been invited into the place of hurt, things begin to change. In many ways, the prophetic voice is akin to prayer—we are speaking to God and listening to His voice on behalf of a person or situation. We are asking God to do the supernatural on behalf of others who often aren't even aware of their need. Don't connect the prophetic voice to Ezekiel or Jeremiah. No camel hair clothing or doomsday proclamations over a city. We are simply listening for God's heart toward a person or situation. The prophetic voice is not one of direction, but affirmation. Not foretelling the future, but confirming present grace.

I've found that my own brokenness in certain areas keeps me from hearing the truth of God when I need it most. It's called a blind spot. Everyone can see it but me. This is why the prophetic voice is so valuable. Another person is able to see broken areas, fractures in my soul, that I don't necessarily know I have. When I allow those I'm walking with to address these places of brokenness, they are able to bring God-healing and gospel-wholeness to me that I wasn't even aware I needed.

Most believers have had some sort of experience with the prophetic voice. If you immediately push back on that idea, perhaps it's simply because that's not language you use. That's OK. But we've all had moments of intuition, or had a godly hunch about someone or some situation. We have accidently seen behind the curtain of a person's heart for just a moment. We have seen something we weren't supposed to see. Shame was revealed. Addiction showed itself. We seemed to sense that something was not right. We have all had the experience of seeing what was hidden. Perhaps a verse of scripture comes to mind for someone. We remember a story that we know will incline someone's heart toward repentance and redemption. Perhaps our hearts just break over another's pain. God uses all things. The longer we walk with the Spirit of God, the more often we find that inklings and instincts give way to the truth that God is present and ready to go to work on our behalf. The prophetic voice is ready to speak to a broken situation; but first the ear is busy listening to what God is saying about this person he loves.

Years ago, Amy and I took one of those personality profile tests. You're probably familiar with them. Myers Briggs, Strength Finders, Enneagram, DISC assessments—they go by a dozen different names. They help you identify how you're made and what your emotional tendencies are. People typically take them when entering a new company or interviewing for a different vocation. In this particular test we were taking, all of the personalities were described as types of tools. That is, some people were labeled as screwdrivers; others were duct tape. Some were wrenches. Amy and I met with the person administering the test, and he was surprised about our results. We were hammers. Both of us. The evaluator explained that married couples typically have complementary personalities. Not us. He explained that our basic tendency as hammers would be to treat every other person and every situation like—you guessed it—like a nail. We laughed. The evaluator did not laugh. He explained that, as is true with all personality types, there are positive and negative aspects to those who are hammers. He warned us that we needed to be intent on keeping our hearts tender toward God, lest we begin to see everyone around us as someone to be conquered or to compete with. We heeded the counselor's advice and began to allow others into this bent of our hearts. We confessed this propensity to those with whom we were doing life, and they just laughed and nodded. Because of course, they already knew we were hammers.

I guess that's how it usually works. We're the last ones to see our own frailties, and then we wonder, "Why has no one ever told me?" This is why cultivating a prophetic voice in community is so important. Otherwise everyone sits around as bystanders watching a potential train wreck. The prophetic voice has the responsibility to call people out of dark places. Like John the Baptist calling the remnant of Israel to the Messiah, we are prophets to our own people—calling them to grace and wholeness in Christ. We must remember that we are not calling others to community, but to Christ first in community. There is a difference. Community is not the end goal. Christ is the goal. Christ in community.

Those who speak with this kind of holy listening may be welcomed. Not always though. It makes no difference. The people of Judah threw Jeremiah into a well when he told them how long their Babylonian captivity would last. The Apostle John was exiled to Patmos because of his loving rebuke to an empire. Our role in deep friendship is to deliver the message of grace, with grace. This requires a listening heart and an ear bent to the Holy Spirit. "He whose ear listens to careful words spoken will live among the wise" (Proverbs 15:31, New Life Version).

We want to be wise, but the writer makes it clear that careful words are the key. "He whose ear listens to careful words spoken . . ." Our communities don't need more advice givers. Dear Abby is not invited into what we're cultivating. What our friendships require are hope-givers. Grace-givers. Light-bearers. Listeners.

And yet it is not enough to simply listen and tell others what we think. We need the heart of God and the words of God for those enslaved to the past. A hearty dose of scripture, prayer, godly counsel, and compassion all blend together in the prophetic voice.

THE SHARP EDGE OF LOVE

Another important tool is the tool of correction. Let's go ahead and acknowledge that this is a tool we would prefer to never use—and we certainly don't want anyone else to use it on us! We tend to prefer 1000 ignorant fans, but we fear one honest friend. However, friendship is predicated on gospel honesty. Plain honesty is not enough. How many times have you heard someone say, I know I'm unforgiving and judgmental and kind of a jerk. This is just the way I am! But at least I'm honest! Nobody needs that kind of honesty. An honesty that isn't governed by grace isn't really worth the words. It becomes the trademark for the insecure and angry. Gospel honesty, however, is spoken through the lens of God's best and Jesus' plan revealed in Scripture. It is a counter-intuitive honesty that understands what is to be spoken and what is to be withheld. Maturity puts a govern over our heart and tongue. This move toward gospel honesty also makes us dreadfully aware of our own fractured hearts—it makes us careful not to project our own judgements or weakness or frailties on another.

It is worth noting that we should be hesitant to use this tool. Correction should not be the first thing we grab in this journey of spiritual repair. Correction is a scalpel. It cuts with precision. But in the hand of someone careless, correction wounds rather than heals.

More often, however, our reticence in applying correction is rooted in fear. We think our action will be perceived as hypocrisy and judgment. And it may be. We can't control what others think and how they respond. We steel our hearts and pursue peace and holiness on behalf of others because we believe that without peace and holiness "no one will see the Lord" (Hebrews 12:14). We remind ourselves that correction is compassion on display. "Wounds from a friend can be trusted" (Proverbs 27:6). Correction says, I love you enough to hurt you.

Correction is a wound. Make no mistake. But like the wound given by a physician on the operating table, so gospel correction is a wound that is given to heal. In community, we identify spiritual cancer and are intent on inflicting even more pain so that true healing can be possible. We are not masochistic. It gives us no joy to see others in pain. We are intent on their lasting joy. This is the purpose of the tool of correction. "Brothers and sisters, if someone is caught in a sin, you who live by the Spirit should restore that person gently. But watch yourselves, or you also may be tempted. Carry each other's burdens, and in this way you will fulfill the law of Christ" (Galatians 6:1–2).

Correction doesn't happen in a vacuum. Catching someone in a sin implies policing the people of God. Big brother replacing a loving father is not what we are after. Correction happens only after seeing the arc of a behavior over the long run.

On any given day you may see me in line at Starbucks. Most days I am patient and kind and I wait my turn. I am keenly aware that those behind the counter are doing their best, and I am simply one of a thousand customers they will serve. I get my coffee and walk away, thankful that my caffeine addiction has been satisfied. However, what if one day you walk into Starbucks and see me angrily impatient with my wife and snippy with the barista? What if you see me walk out of Starbucks huffing that my

Americano is not to my liking? What would you do? What should you do? Am I walking in entitlement? Or am I just having a bad day? It's hard to know the difference if we only know people at a distance.

We can't judge others based on their worst days. If you were to see me in my most fragile, broken, and hopeless moments, you might wonder if I am even a Christian. Seriously. I do not always behave Christian-ly. Gratefully, in my brokenness I am most aware of the love of God, but I am also keenly aware of my weakness. This is why God gives us new mercy every morning. He gives us the strength to cling to his sufficiency, and the grace so that we might give the benefit of the doubt to those who are struggling.

This is why correction is designed to be administered in community, because these are the people who know us best. We can't fake it with those who see us week in and week out. You can cover over your frailties in an auditorium with hundreds of other worshippers, but not with the 10-12 you gather with on Wednesday nights. You can feign depth as you watch a webcast of a TV preacher, but that's not real. Superficial, high-tech, hyper-edited and smoke machine spirituality will never get you to the finish line of faith. The reason? There is no one there to correct you, help you, uphold you, and spur you on to be who God made you to be. "No discipline seems pleasant at the time, but painful. Later on, however, it produces a harvest of righteousness and peace for those who have been trained by it" (Hebrews 12:11).

There are two primary reasons that so little correction happens in the church. First, there are so few who are in deep, long-lasting relationship with others who can see the long arc of life, thereby enabling them to identify a need for correction. Second, most people lack the required courage. I'm not throwing stones—I am cowardly in this department. More often than not, we bow to the belief that it is unloving to correct someone's behavior. Even if there is longevity in relationship, we tend to believe that many friends will breed natural accountability. But that's just not true. Unless a person's unhealthy or sinful behavior directly and negatively affects our lives, we make a sweeping internal assumption that someone else will help them or correct them or confront them when needed. Unfortunately, everyone is making that assumption and those around us shipwreck their lives with a hundred spectators in view. Generally, this is when a great cry arises, an indictment to church leaders, that they weren't doing their job.

This tool of correction requires some finesse. As you can imagine, timing is everything. The setting matters too. This is why Jesus is so careful to describe it in Matthew 18. "If your brother sins against you, go and tell him his fault, between you and him alone. If he listens to you, you have gained your brother. But if he does not listen, take one or two others along with you, that every charge may be established by the evidence of two or three witnesses. If he refuses to listen to them, tell it to the church. And if he refuses to listen even to the church, let him be to you as a Gentile and a tax collector" (vv. 15–17). This text feels hard and harsh, doesn't it? It's helpful to remind ourselves that real love does hard things. Real love embraces the inconvenience of having hard conversations because people's lives and marriages and hearts are on the line.

MAKING THE TURN

I proudly drive an 18-year-old jalopy. It limps along our city streets, but it eventually gets me where I need to go. My wife drives the newer car. I don't begrudge her for it. I love what I drive, mostly because it has a story. We've had this car for a large portion of our marriage. It was shiny and (almost) new when we got it. We've driven it across the country and it held both of our babies. Hundreds of errands have been run in this gem. Both of my children learned to drive in my car. This car has history with us. The new car smell faded many years ago and has now been replaced with something that can only be described as fermented peanut butter and jelly. Several years ago, she (yes, my car has a gender!) started making some pretty serious noises under the hood. Dings and booms and rat-a-tat-tats. Those were my descriptions to the mechanic. I even tried to mimic the noises with my mouth. He wasn't interested. It turned out she needed an overhaul. A new engine. We were told we could either sell the car for parts or re-invest. We ponied up the cash and now she drives like new again.

I tell you that story because the costliest tool in the toolbox of community is repentance—a call to spiritual overhaul. There is no way to overstate the power of this tool. It's more than simple confession. And it costs more than vulnerability. It carries with it the tenor of humility, and yet feels like a call to die. Cross-carrying and clarion cries to lay down every right. A call to repentance is the plea to leave the "cares of the world and the deceitfulness of riches and the desires for other things . . ." (Mark 4:19) and pursue the new life of wholeness found in Christ. Repentance is hard—impossible, in fact, without the work of the Holy Spirit. Repentance, however, is the cornerstone of faith in Christ and community. Without repentance all we have is politically-driven, emotionally-charged, biblically hypocritical groups of people who aren't really interested in deep community, but rather, in whitewashed behavior. The ability to abide with Jesus, settle in with others, and walk humbly for a lifetime is dependent on active repentance.

"But this is how God fulfilled what he had foretold through all the prophets, saying that his Messiah would suffer. Repent, then, and turn to God, so that your sins may be wiped out, that times of refreshing may come from the Lord" (Acts 3:18–19). The tool of repentance is made to incline our hearts to God. Because repentance is first about God. In fact, repentance is primarily about God. And yet most of our sin appears, at least on the surface, to be horizontal in nature. We sin against our spouse or child. We sin against our body or time. We sin against a co-worker or creation. And while sin has horizontal consequences, it finds its fundamental consequence in heaven and our relationship with the Creator. We sin first against God, then people. The sin of adultery, for example, is first an offense to the One who made marriage holy. The sin of gluttony is first a sin against the One who made our bodies and called them good. The sin of neglect is first a sin against the One who called us to number our days. Sin is first an offense to God. Because of this reality, repentance must be directed to God first. Our loving confrontation in human relationship is first a call to be reconciled to our Father in heaven, then reconciled with people and circumstances.

Repentance is about restoration as well. "If someone falls into sin, forgivingly restore him . . ." (Galatians 6:1, The Message). It is no small thing to take a broken heart and restore it. It requires a safe place, long suffering, and compassion. By now, I hope, we have moved into a place of community where this call to repentance is not only possible, but welcomed. Those who know they are trapped in sin crave a change in mind and affection. The Psalmist understood this longing for repentance. "As a deer pants for flowing streams, so pants my soul for you, O God. My soul thirsts for God, for the living God. When shall I come and appear before God? My tears have been my food day and night, while they say to me all the day long, "Where is your God?" (Psalm 42:1–3).

Some rebellious souls run headlong into sin. Others fall into it. As humans we are all sinners (Romans 3:23). Rebellious even. But most men and women I know have a keen desire to live well. They want their lives to matter. They want to raise their kids with an awareness of God's heart for creation and the world around them. Most want to use their vocation as a platform to honor Jesus. Most people I know draw a circle around their lives and say, "This little piece of real estate will bring honor to God. That's my promise today." We all want our lives to have weight to them. We don't want to live for small ambitions. But we often do.

Drifting has become the acceptable form of sin—the gray area of sin perhaps. If only those we were walking with were making black tar heroin in their spare bedroom, we might have an open-and-shut case to call them to repentance. Instead what we notice, what becomes most evident, is a hardness of heart. A cooling of affections to the things of God. An indifference to who they were made to be. Drifting is a dangerous sin. Maybe the most dangerous.

Community calls our friends back from the edges. Not that Sunday sermons and weekend environments can't compel. We hope they do. But we know these people. We're able to notice when a distance grows in their marriage; the warning signs are subtle, but clear that they are just parroting the right spiritual words but covering over a hard heart. We see that work has taken preeminence over the much needed soul margin. We get a little worried when they spend more weekends at the lake than with the people of God. We get that holy nudge from the Spirit that something is amiss. This is the moment that most will echo the words of Cain, "Am I my brother's keeper?" And the answer is yes. We are. Their holiness is their responsibility, but it's often our privilege to call it out. A relationship with God is deeply personal, but meant to be lived out communally.

Calling others to repentance requires courage. And courage is best practiced in community with others. Again, Matthew 18 gives us a grace-saturated mechanism in restoring someone to wholeness.

1. Go to them individually. They are our people after all. Honor them as people first. No need to ambush them by bringing reinforcements. "Hey Stan, can we grab a cup of coffee? I love you and I'm worried about you." Repentance is always about love.

2. If they fail to repent, take someone with you. Not because the person you bring with you will have wise and crafty arguments, but because the person in sin needs to see how their sin affects the community. My sin is your sin. Your restoration is my restoration. "I brought Allen with me because the three of us have been through it together. You know we would walk over hot coals for you."

3. If they continue in their hard-heartedness, take them before their community. This isn't public corporal punishment. Thirty-nine lashes will not be given. Transparency in the family is what we're after. This

step toward restoration is painful but necessary to give people a clear picture of how powerful community can and should be. Their heart and wholeness is worth the seriousness of this moment. "We have met with Stan. He's in a painful and destructive season in his life. We're bringing him to you, our community, because you know him and love him. Please call him. Text him. Have him over for dinner."

4. If they still fail to embrace freedom, we're commanded to treat them like an unbeliever. So how do we treat an unbeliever? We all have an itchy trigger finger with the judgment gun. Before we shoot the wounded, perhaps we should first look through the lens of grace, gospel, and redemption. How are we to treat unbelievers? How did Jesus treat those far from grace? He ate with them, spent enormous amounts of time with them, and loved them in ways that made religious elites squirm. In other words, if someone in our community rejects the call to wholeness, we don't reject them or excommunicate them. We double down on love. After all, they are people who are made in the image of God. Intrinsically valuable. Loved and pursued by the Creator of the universe. Ransomed at Calvary. Real people to be restored gently—not taught a lesson. We treat unbelievers with respect and love and pursue them the way Jesus pursues us.

APPLICATION

Joe and Patty have been a test case in putting this into practice. It has been a whirlwind of listening, correcting, and repenting. And then repeating it for good measure. It turns out that this thing of personal holiness and maturity isn't a one-and-done sort of business. We listen and then listen some more. We receive feedback and correction and then we drift . . . again. A kind word of correction is offered after what seems like hours of listening and encouraging. Repentance is celebrated. Or it should be. Then we drift some more and are once again thrown a life preserver of grace and friendship. This feels like the cult classic movie Groundhog Day. Over and over and over again, only to find out this is the pattern and practice of people that truly walk together. It's work. A good work. A Godly work. A work that we can enjoy together. But still, it's work. We repent. We own where we have failed. In fact, grace calls us to own more than our fair share. We open our heart to wounding, because these wounds can be trusted. We set our expectations and eyes on the one who restores. Not on the people—we will disappoint and be disappointed. But the one who puts all things back together is forever faithful and he is the one in whom we place our full trust.

1. Make a list of friendships that have disintegrated over the course of your adult life. Then identify where you were responsible for the breakdown of trust and longevity.
2. Write three emails today to people in your life who you have hurt as a result of your brokenness and selfishness. Ask them to forgive you for contributing to the fracture of your friendship.
3. Host a dinner with a family or friend with whom you wish a relationship were restored.
4. Invite your community to share their stories in which they have experienced relational fracture.
5. Do a bible study in which you record places in the bible in which relationships were restored (i.e. Jesus and Peter, Paul and John Mark, etc . . .)

7

The Bedroom is for Covenant

PASTORS, BY WAY OF expectation, marry people. The church I serve has lots of young adults who are in love, and that means I do lots of weddings. Before the vows are ever spoken or the teal bridesmaid's dresses are ever donned, pre-marital counseling happens. These meetings usually take place in my office, and a big part of my job is to try to prepare this rose-colored couple for a reality that rarely includes a romantic soundtrack. Marriage, I tell them, is full of work, laundry, learning, and fighting. But mostly, just lots of just showing up. I stare at these "kids" who are deeply and amorously in love. I expect them to balk at my warning that one day they will face enormous conflict. I double down in telling them there will be days, hopefully in the far distant future, when it will require a colossal amount of grace and energy just to stay in it. They roll their eyes at this declaration. Groom-to-be pats wife-to-be's hand and whispers to her that life together will always be romantic and easy.

I throw up in my mouth a little. I know better.

I lean in, on the edge of my chair now, and reassure them that while their marriage may be romantic and beautiful and unpredictable in the first years, they will most likely settle into something all-together different as times goes on. I divulge to them that love changes over time. I say it as if I am telling them a secret. And then the next part of the conversation is what really surprises young couples. I tell them that their marriage will be much better in twenty years (or at least, it should be!) I repeat it a few times and raise my voice for emphasis. They are visibly confused now. Your marriage may not be starry-eyed and hormonal in two decades, but it will be good—really good. There's a depth that is only possible with time and testing and pain. And it will be even better in 30 years. I tell them that the meat of marriage is found in the mundane of routine and faithfulness.

CONSUMMATION OF ALL THINGS

Naked, transparent, unrelenting faith is what is celebrated in the bedroom of the house of community. Now before your mind wanders and you begin to think this is about to get kinky, just remember that this is all metaphor. Each room represents a place of greater meaning, deeper friendship, and healthier hearts. While we all begin in the foyer, our hope is to end up in the bedroom. That is, if the foyer is the place for new introductions and shallow connections, then the bedroom is the place of relational consummation. Like in marriage, the bedroom represents the place of covenant. We can walk an aisle and repeat vows, but until the marriage is consummated, we are not yet one.

So what do I mean by consummation? While every metaphor eventually breaks down (certainly this one does), the communal consummation is what we are after. Nobody wants one more shallow relationship. And no one wants to be engaged forever. Marriage is what we are made for. Even the language of the kingdom of God arcs towards this bride/groom tenor. "Let us rejoice and be glad and give him glory! For the wedding of the Lamb has come, and his bride has made herself ready. Fine linen, bright and clean, was given her to wear. Then the angel said to me, 'Write this: Blessed are those who are invited to the wedding supper of the Lamb!' And he added, 'These are the true words of God'" (Revelation 19:7–9). Consummation is first a kingdom reality, then a relational one. We are first made one with God, through Jesus, and then brought into oneness with others. This was the Apostle Paul's great aim that we all walk in "the ministry of reconciliation" (2 Corinthians 5:18).

Covenant is the language of a community that sticks together. After we have sat around a table; after learning to walk in the middle space of life; and after all the communal naysayers have finished watching to see if it was real— covenant keepers step forward. We're not talking about contracts., but rather, covenant. If/then relationships don't last long under duress. Covenant, however, is a bond born of a promise, not of negotiation. God says in the New Covenant that our sin is no longer held against us (Romans 6:14) because of the persistent, ferocious, and eternal love of another. He says, "This is what I will do, no matter what." Contract says, "If you do this, then I will do that. If you don't follow through on your end, all bets are off!"

Deep gospel community is first a covenant with God who makes and keeps his promises to us. Make no mistake, we need someone in our relationships to be the promise keeper. We like to think of ourselves as faithful, but our hearts will fail. He will always come through; always forgive; always draw near; always comfort. It is in God's nature to make promises and to keep them for his glory. He was a promise keeper to Adam and Eve—their brokenness would not end in ultimate death, but God would redeem them through an heir (Genesis 3:16–17). God made a promise to Noah by way of an ark and a rainbow (Genesis 9:8–17). God made a promise to Abraham that his family would be a blessing to all the nations (Genesis 12:1–3). God made a promise to Moses that the law would be inscribed on the hearts of all people (Exodus 19:1–24). God promised David that his throne would never end (1 Chronicles 17:11–14). And God makes a promise to us, via the cross of Jesus—we are put into a family. We are now sons and daughters of a perfect father; brothers and sisters walking together in freedom and relationship. Despite our past failures or future foibles, we are invited, included, pursued, and presented into the family of God because of the promise of the cross. There is nothing that can change the covenant that God makes with his people.

A NOD TO COVENANT PROBLEMS

This beautiful idea of a being a covenant people with God is perfect and full. But being a covenant people with one another has a few problems. Gospel covenant first is born out of the larger storyline of scripture in which we see God choosing a people for himself. He could have chosen any nation on planet earth, and yet he chose one. A people for himself (1 Peter 2:9). We should rejoice and be glad in this large family of God with Jesus at the center. But because we are slow to learn and naturally employ a debtor's ethic in our relationships (you do for me then I do for you), our covenants often end up looking very similar to contracts.

Because of that, it seems helpful to simply acknowledge the breakdown of language and application within the human experience of covenant—that is, we must admit that we do this poorly. We are not good at this. The first and most obvious problem is that you and I are not God. I would imagine you don't need someone to remind you of that. Or maybe you do. Lots of days I forget I am not in charge and sovereign over my life. This reminder helps us understand how powerful the covenant God makes with humans really is.

Over and over in the scripture we see clearly how God is the only one who can truly fulfill a covenant. In fact, in the Old Testament a common practice among men in making a covenant with one another would seem barbaric to us today. A bull would be slaughtered and its body parts laid alongside each other, leaving just enough room for a narrow walkway. Each man in the covenant would then ceremonially walk between the shed blood, and in doing so, a covenant (the blood of a bull) was made and was considered unbreakable.

God, in making a covenant with Abraham, invited him into this special relationship. "'Bring me a heifer three years old, a female goat three years old, a ram three years old, a turtledove, and a young pigeon.' And he brought him all these, cut them in half, and laid each half over against the other . . . As the sun was going down, a deep sleep fell on Abram . . . When the sun had gone down and it was dark, behold, a smoking fire pot and a flaming torch passed between these pieces. On that day the Lord made a covenant with Abram" (Genesis 15:9–10, 12, 17–18). Notice that only One walked through the pathway of covenant. Abraham is made to sleep. Only one is able to make the promise to fully walk in integrity, always walk in relationship, eternally walk in love. Of course, this is a foreshadow of the cross of Christ and his promise of new covenant with us. We are unable to bear the weight of eternal faithfulness in our own strength. And yet God invites us into this unbreakable blood covenant and fulfills all the requirements through the substitutionary work of Jesus.

The reason creating a community with a covenant mindset is problematic is because we are not even in the same cosmos in regards to the character and immutability of God. We waver often; our fear keeps us from drawing close; we live suspicious of others. But we still make covenants with one another. Imperfect covenants, for sure. With hesitation, and often with an eye on the exit, we say, "I will stay. I will do what is required. I will lay down my rights. When you fail, I will forgive. When you leave, I will pursue. I will fail again and again. But by the grace of God, I'm in this for the long haul." Again, imperfectly we do this. I can't underscore this enough. We are not good at covenant, but our hearts are made for it. That is problem number one.

Problem number two is similar, but enough different that it is worth mentioning. We live in a modern culture that wars against what we're trying to build. Developed cultures like ours prefer contract living. Covenant is just too old fashioned for our time. It feels like something someone might agree to if they had no other options. For example, travel is a relatively new invention in the human experience. For most of human history (outside of the last 100 years), people were born, lived, and died pretty much in the same place. Not because humans didn't have an innate desire to explore the world, but the means to do so were unavailable. But now with the advent of relatively cheap travel a person can explore each corner of the world. In fact, it is expected that you and I should travel, move around, and make our mark on this vast earth. In extreme cases, we pity those who have never crossed state lines and at the very least, we wonder why our friends settle for less by staying put.

The reason this is problematic is obvious: people leave. They come and go. The idea of staying anywhere has been erased from the 21st century ethos. The belief of driving roots down deep with a company or in marriage or in community is quickly becoming foreign to a younger population. As we do the work of building a community, we discover that not everyone will stay—in fact, most won't. Some leave because it's too hard. Others because the diversity makes them uncomfortable. Some simply leave a community because the idea of staying anywhere for too long seems too ordinary, too boring. They hear the echo of the latest commercial, "Be different. Go big!" and they leave. This makes building something of substance and something sustainable increasingly more challenging.

Staying is How We Win

Covenant is long-term. When I say long-term, what I hope for and dream of is lifetime covenant. Two becoming one. Friendships and families bound together. Single moms and solitary living being replaced by a greater vision for love. Covenant is a binding together that is more attractive than en vogue radical individualism. We are not meant to undo what God puts together. There's no undoing oneness.

Because there is often no watershed moment in marriage or friendship or community, it's usually just doing lots of forgetful things together over decades of time. These sacred seconds, dedicated to God over years, are what drive us deeper. Not that there aren't moments that mark us, scar us—the death of a child, the loss of a job, the breakdown of a body. These are all serious things that take our breath away. But those big moments are dwarfed in the light of decades of just staying . . . of persevering.

The bible calls this faithfulness. It is a cornerstone characteristic of God. He stays. He is faithful even when we are not faithful (2 Timothy 2:13). No matter our faithlessness, no matter how our affections cool, he is true to us. He puts his faithfulness on display for all creation by coming in pursuit of a broken people. He knows we don't have what it takes to finish well on our own. Intrinsically, we lack follow-through. We don't have stick-to-it-ness. Something else drives us—usually broken ambition. People pleasing, too.

When I counsel Christian couples who are contemplating divorce, I remind them in no uncertain terms that divorce is not a viable option. I don't mean to sound bullyish. That is never my intention with couples. But I like to remind them that God has been faithful to them. He covenanted with each of them to be faithful to them in marriage. To undo what God has done is no small thing. They may be unhappy, hurt, and tired, but those feelings (as real as they are), are always secondary to covenant. God has bound two people together "for better or for worse." We are a people firstly bound to what God has done. As long as God continues to keep his promise, which he has, we lose the right to step outside of that covenant. This is why couples who stay—who fight through the tears and hold on to the One who doesn't change—often come through stronger and more resilient. Covenant has that effect on us. It anchors us to bedrock. It keeps us bound to where life is true.

Open This Gift Slowly

Pain is always present in covenant. One does not beget the other. This is just an observation—when people are bound together, pain is present. Mostly because pain is everywhere people have put their feet. We live in a timeline marred by this curse. And yet community, this ancient covenant, is often forged in the furnace of pain. Pain is a gift in that way. The ancient theology of suffering causes our minds to drift to the stories of Job and Jeremiah. Patmos Island and upside-down crosses. Pain is not something we sign up for. It finds us and grabs us with all its vigor and demands our undivided attention. We prefer other doctrines for sure, knowing this is no feel good creed. Make no mistake, pain is coming whether we are in community or not. Pain, like the changing seasons, is a guarantee.

"In this world you will have trouble" (John 16:33). We hold this promise loosely, knowing that resurrection is around the corner. Death is imminent, but God is preeminent. Suffering is inevitable, but it will be swallowed up by the glory of God. Pain looks like it rules the day, but it is only a lesser god to the One who rules all things.

This is what we parrot when the waters are calm. But when life swoons, we often question the motives of our Father. A heart whisper asks, Is God good? Can he truly love me and also ordain this suffering? How in the world could this loss ever bring God glory? Heartache often triggers a heart drift. This is why we need community to anchor us when the winds blow. We need people to remind us that pain—this gift—is designed to draw us to a comforting Father, not to push us away. The gift of pain produces "endurance, and endurance produces character, and character produces hope, and hope does not put us to shame" (Romans 5:3). This gift we do not want is how we grow.

For this reason, pain is not the enemy of life, though we unquestionably live like it is. We run from pain into the arms of pointless pleasure. We medicate pain with media or chocolate cake. But pain is only a medium. It has no personal ethic. There is no good pain or bad pain. Just pain. It reveals what is hidden in dark places. It is an amplifier to our souls. If we are alone, pain will reveal how alone we are. If we are indifferent in our faith, pain will reveal the great chasm that separates religion from intimacy. But when crisis comes and we are in deep, bedroom kinds of community, pain will not be the only voice speaking. Pain may mute our cries, but it does nothing to the faith of those around us. They shout for us. They sing for us. They pray for us. We hold onto their faith when our faith feels like it is failing.

A covenant community is worth its weight in gold when life falls apart. It is in these times that our people remind us of what is true, because pain lies. In these moments when the wind of the storm is deafening, our people anchor us from wandering onto the rocks. When we don't have words to pray, except tears and contempt, our people pray for us.

Pain will shape us, but it should not define us. Those men and women walking alongside us will gently whisper that our defeat is always redeemable in the economy of God. They will direct our hearts to God's mercy, knowing his tenderness is most acute in the face of our deepest hurt. Our friends by our side will hold us and carry us to the healer. They will dig a hole in a roof, if need be, knowing he is present. The greatest message of pain—this thing that our community repeats to us—is that this life is a mist. A vapor. We need to hear all of these things from those we trust. They don't speak these words all at once, of course. Sometimes in the midst of tragedy and pain, no words are needed (Job 13:5). But real community does eventually speak.

"Praise be to the God and Father of our Lord Jesus Christ, the Father of compassion and the God of all comfort, who comforts us in all our troubles, so that we can comfort those in any trouble with the comfort we ourselves receive from God. For just as we share abundantly in the sufferings of Christ, so also our comfort abounds through Christ" (2 Corinthians 1:3–5). Our people speak life and truth and grace and hope. Hallmark greeting card comfort is not what is needed when life fractures. The potency of resurrection and the insurmountable sovereignty of God is what will ultimately bring comfort to soul scars. The hope that the suffering in this life is not worth comparing to the glory that will one day be revealed (Romans 8:18) is the cornerstone we build our lives on, the foundation we build our community on.

All that God has, he shares with his children. And that includes his suffering. Even Jesus "learned obedience by what he suffered" (Hebrews 5:8). Paul counted it an honor to "suffer disgrace for the Name" (Acts 5:41). James counted it all joy to suffer (James 1:2). As we share in the sufferings of Christ, it enables comfort to flow. Great need always precedes great mercy. And this is why the community of Jesus is so powerful. The words of life and comfort flow through us, the dwellings of the Holy Spirit. We need each other in the worst times of life so that we can experience the most important comfort our souls are made for.

COVENANT AUTHORITY

"Submit to one another out of reverence for Christ" (Ephesians 5:21). Authority always flows out of a covenant relationship. Not power, but authority. A man with a gun may have power. But a policeman with a badge has authority. One is operating out of fear and isolation, the other is operating out of covenant with a community.

Jesus spoke with authority (Matthew 7:29). He spoke with authority because he operated out of authority. He knew who he was, what he was. "All authority in heaven and on earth has been given to me" (Matthew 28:18). Jesus had power too. He had power to raise the dead and heal the sick and ruin a funeral. But his power was rooted in his authority as the Son of God.

It appears Jesus had no problem operating in authority because he was first under authority. "Truly, truly, I say to you, the Son can do nothing of his own accord, but only what he sees the Father doing. For whatever the Father does, that the Son does likewise" (John 5:19). Jesus was no rogue. He joyfully submitted to the Father. There was a freedom in it.

Earlier, I mentioned that I tell couples that divorce is never an option when their marriage is on the rocks. I also tell them that in the midst of their personal tsunami, when the knee-jerk reaction of pain is to leave, they need to trust someone in authority. We ask them to submit. Staying together is hard enough. Then add the outdated, archaic word submit. Our imagination drifts to ancient caves of the Middle East as tribal leaders shout threats to underlings.

However submission has been subjugated by culture, it is a beautiful kingdom reality that we are meant to enjoy, not endure. It's the twin-sister of surrender. Hands lifted high and voice shouting, "I give up!" Couples in trouble need someone to guide them in the storm. They don't know up from down. The pain and loss and arguing has created a cyclone that has made life go sideways. What they need is someone to bring clarity and anchor them to spiritual bedrock. This is what gospel authority does. It sees for the blind. It hears for the deaf. It leads them to still waters.

Deep and alive community is not a destination. You don't arrive there. You fight for it. You hope and pray for the right people, spend more time than you can afford, expose the darkest places of your heart, repent in critical moments, allow others to speak truth and direction into your life . . . and then you wait. You're waiting to see if this authority you have given them is reciprocated. Will they give the permission that is required that makes community dangerously beautiful? Will they allow you to speak and demonstrate with authority in their lives?

Pastors are often given this gift by the people they shepherd. Not always, but sometimes. This authority is given in the most critical times of life. Funerals and weddings. Hospitals and cancer. Lost jobs and messy divorces. Pastors are given unbelievable power to speak the most difficult things and be thanked for it. This is a rare time when position intersects authority. But authority is not bound to position. In fact, many in positions of power have no real authority. And those in authority often have no position. But when you find yourself in community that is healthy and good and life-giving, you willingly give this gift to those who hold no position except that of friend.

The natural question arises, what are we giving others the authority to do?

First, we give our community the authority to confirm the direction of our lives.

"Now in the church at Antioch there were prophets and teachers: Barnabas, Simeon called Niger, Lucius of Cyrene, Manaen (who had been brought up with Herod the tetrarch) and Saul. While they were worshiping the Lord and fasting, the Holy Spirit said, 'Set apart for me Barnabas and Saul for the work to which I have called them.' So after they had fasted and prayed, they placed their hands on them and sent them off" (Acts 13:1–3). Barnabas and Paul leveraged the authority of friendship. Acts 13 is not the description of an anemic little church community, but a vivid replay of the authority of friendship to affirm calling.

Calling is not new to modern day saints. Direction in life, the ever elusive will of God, is something we have all wondered if we have truly discovered. Especially with nuanced verses like Romans 12:2, "Then you will be able to test and approve what God's will is—his good, pleasing and perfect will." At first glance, we think that there is a God's will that is good. And then there is a God's will that is perfect. I definitely want the perfect will of God. Right? We are a fickle people; recklessly, we label a heart-whim or personal desire as "God's will." This is dangerous and silly and immature. Thank God we have a community that discerns along with us what God's will actually is for our lives.

This was true in Antioch. Saul and Barnabas needed others who could speak with authority, hear the voice of God, and say for certain what was true. Saul and Barnabas were already leaders, pastors in this church. Certainly they didn't need anyone's permission to go and plant other churches. Authority has less to do with permission and more to do with self-awareness. That is, when we submit to the authority of others, we are making the confession, My heart is prone to wander. I don't always choose the best and right things. So I need more eyes, more ears listening for God with me, on account of me.

Authority can speak hard things. And good things. And dangerous things.

Remember, when God spoke, creation happened. The authority we give creates life when used appropriately.

I have a friend named Valentino. When he met the young lady who would eventually become his wife, he fell deeply in love. But he was unsure if he could trust his feelings. He had a checkered track record when it came to women. By this time, he was walking with Jesus and didn't want to marry someone out of loneliness or insecurity. Valentino was also walking in deep community with a few other men, and he did the unspeakable—he gave these men authority to speak into his love life. Before you start thinking the worst, this had nothing to do with control or manipulation. These men had no interest in pulling the strings in a fledgling relationship. They had their own lives and families to lead. What Valentino asked them to do was fast and pray with him for 21 days. He wanted to know God's heart. He asked these men to evaluate, with love, his motives and frailties, and ask God with him if he was ready for marriage, and if the woman he was dating was the woman he should pursue covenant with. Valentino gave these men authority to speak weighty things in his life. During those 21 days, these men were able to address some painful areas in which Valentino needed to grow and submit to God. Because of Valentino's willing submission to authority in deep community, their listening ears and grace-filled mouths were joyful confirmations to what Valentino felt deeply in his heart.

If you cringe at that story, it is likely because you have embraced American individualism. It has seeped into the life of church community as well. We may appreciate advice or feedback or instruction, but ultimately our business is our business. We say and believe that it's our prerogative if we choose to divorce a spouse or file for bankruptcy or put a second mortgage on our house. In reality, we have relegated our gospel community to the background task of mere comforters, and we have castrated our people of their role as counselors. But a Jesus-centered, gracious, patient, and merciful authority over our lives is one of the greatest gifts we can receive in community. It has the potential to save us from the worst decisions. Even more, however, our community has the privilege of praying and standing and even sending us on mission, if we will let them.

We must learn to leverage our deep gospel friendships. We can no longer sit by and watch as those in the family of Jesus shipwreck their lives on the rocks of this world. Debt, divorce, adultery, idolatry, and pornography are all things we must speak into. We don't dance around what is most dangerous. We don't recommend they simply read a book or take a class that will help them deal with their issues. We are their community. So we speak with authority. We have put in the time and investment. These are our people. You have their ears. This doesn't mean you shout like an Old Testament prophet, but the urgency of your message is no less weighty.

Every family, every member of your community needs someone to speak with authority over their lives. We must speak the hard things—Stop working so much . . . Hey, your children should not be the focus of your family—that's idolatry, and your children are lousy gods . . . Let's work on body image together . . . It's not OK to talk about your husband or wife that way . . . It seems that your heart is drifting from God.

Jeremiah and Ezekiel were both prophets during the Babylonian exile. One was in Jerusalem and one was in exile with the people. We are to play both parts in the life of community. We are Jeremiahs, reminding people of what could be, what should be. We don't live in exile forever. We stand outside their lives with a heavenward perspective, reminding them of what is coming through God's faithfulness.

But we are also Ezekiels. Incarnation in exile. Life has not worked out like we thought it would. It is community in crisis. Ezekiels are those who speak painfully and authoritatively in the most difficult times. Jeremiah was thrown in a well. Ezekiel was never heard from again. But we still speak. Not because we will necessarily be rewarded, but because the words of life reside in our hearts.

There is no room in this kind of community for friends whose talk is as "smooth as butter" (Psalm 55:12). Fraudulent speaking and half-hearted living are no help when what we need is something of substance. Not that we aren't all in process, but spiritual honesty is demanded at this level of relationship. A veneer of faith on a rotting foundation is not going to get anyone to the finish line.

COVENANT BURDEN BEARING

Covenant and authority find their fulfillment in burden bearing. Spiritual muscles are built in this weighty activity—carrying the load for someone else when life falls apart. Single moms, widowed husbands, lost jobs, colicky babies, unexpected funerals, last minute babysitting, and everything in between are burden-bearing opportunities.

Paul gives this dense command to the young church at Galatia, "Bear one another's burdens, and so fulfill the law of Christ" (Galatians 6:2). Not too long ago I read this command and thought, Why does Paul connect this strange theological wing to this idea of burden bearing? That is, why does carrying the weight of others' afflictions fulfill the law of Christ? I believe the Apostle Paul is telling us something about the nature of God. Christ has already fulfilled the law—He has borne our burden. That is, the law in the Old Covenant demanded perfection, which Jesus fulfilled. It is clear, then, that Paul is not telling us to fulfill that law because he knows that is not only an impossibility, but it has already been accomplished.

However, when Christ came to the earth, his perfect life (1 Peter 2:22) was defined by his perfect obedience (Hebrews 5:8) to the law and complete dependence on the Holy Spirit (Luke 4:1). Jesus' gift to us, as part of his redemption, is that he took on himself the absolute burden of the law, and in so doing, he took the burden from us. This is why I ask, What does Paul mean when he says that we fulfill the law of Christ if the law has already been fulfilled?

We find the answer in Matthew 22. Jesus' interaction with an attorney unfolds this way: "'Teacher, which is the greatest commandment in the Law?' Jesus replied: 'Love the Lord your God with all your heart and with all your soul and with all your mind.' This is the first and greatest commandment. And the second is like it: 'Love your neighbor as yourself.' All the Law and the Prophets hang on these two commandments" (Matthew 22:36–40). We find the law of Christ is to love God with all that we are, and to love people in a way that magnifies his worth. This is no small command—a burden in fact. This is why the weightiest and most burdensome of all commands should always be read in light of what Christ has done. In Christ, embracing the power and grace that is now available to every believer, we are truly able to follow the law of Christ. His law is not burdensome, it is a delight. His law is not a millstone hung around our necks for us to sink, but rather, wings with which we soar upon the grace of God. Carrying the weight of my own sin would have been an impossibility, but in light of what Christ has done, I walk free of my past. Bearing the weight of someone else's problems or tragedy or pain is something I would have hated in my former life, but in light of what Christ has done, in taking the tragedy of my life and making it new, I count it a joy.

Naturally, we don't want to bear others' burdens. Inconvenience is our enemy so we resist holding too tightly to the encumbrances of others. Ironically, we cry foul when others don't come around us in our weakness. Burden bearing is a double-edged sword in that way. It requires that we expose our true selves and confess that the lives we portray on our computer screens are not accurate representations of truth. In this place of community, we share our burdens because we are fully aware that we can't carry them on our own. We need God's power and God's people to see God's redemptive work in the hard places of life.

In addition, burden bearing requires regular maintenance on the deep well that is our soul. It's hard to give our best to people and love well when we have nothing to give. When our relationship with God is dry and weak, it is difficult to have empathy for others. When we haven't drunk deeply from the river of living water, what we give others is second hand grace—words that are meant well, but have no real power behind them. Carrying someone else's burden is an impossibility without fresh grace from God, new mercies. Without his mercy, we will be crushed under the weight of disappointment, loss pain, and entitlement. And yet through Jesus' own burden bearing, he now gives us the ability to carry others' burdens, thus, fulfilling his law.

He is our greatest burden bearer. We need him to breathe on our efforts as we choose to do life together in the hard times. No accumulation of good works or great plans can replace the God who can still every storm and right every ship. Burden bearing is the activity of grace received, the mission of God in the middle of broken people.

Burden bearing is hard. And it's work. Both of these are words we isolate from our vocabulary as often as possible. But in the depth of this room, this place of intimacy and honesty and partnership, is the gift we alone can give. Burden-bearing is grace on display. It is our imperfect promise of staying. It is our plea to others to stay, when leaving would be easier. It is giving to another something we are in desperate need for ourselves. We flinch, thinking perhaps we can't afford to give what we need so much of. But the gift of grace which has been so generously poured out for us nudges us to take a chance that this gift is meant to be given, not kept as our own.

APPLICATION

There are no finish lines in this journey of gospel deeps. Yes, heaven. Yes, eternal peace with our Heavenly Father. But in the pursuit of temporal community and friendship and raw family, there is no finish line, only benchmarks. We are able to echo the Apostle Paul, "Not that I have already obtained all this, or have already arrived at my goal, but I press on to take hold of that for which Christ Jesus took hold of me" (Philippians 3:12). Jesus has given us the model and promise of this community we all seek after. We are not chasing after the wind here. This is no dog chasing his tail. Community, like salvation, is a gift to God's people. A life woven together with the fabric of grace and truth and compassion has already been made available to each one of us.

But Paul also acknowledges the effort required. "I do not consider myself yet to have taken hold of it" (v. 13). He knows it has been given to us. It is ours, free and clear. And yet, for most of us, we don't yet have it. A pursuit is necessary. No better verse describes the plight of those who long for this depth of honest, life-giving, and long-term community. We know it has been given to us. We are fully aware we are brothers and sisters born of the same Father. We speak the same language and yearn for the same land, but we are a stiff-necked people and the land is filled with enemies. So we have to take the advice of Paul, "Forget what is behind" (v. 13). That is, don't dwell on every failed attempt. Shout at your fearful heart, "Keep your eyes ahead!" And once again, take hold of the very thing Christ has taken hold of for you. Community is possible. But more importantly, community is waiting for you. You were made for it.

1. Journal about the closest emotional relationship you have experienced. Write about why it was good, what was most challenging and how it was intentionally cultivated.

2. Do a bible word search for *covenant*. Make a list between our covenant with God and our covenant with each other.

3. Invite a friend into deeper relationship by giving them permission to speak into your blind spots and rebellion.

4. Ask your small group, or bible study, or your community to speak into an area in which you need direction. Tell them you are seeking to grow in the area of personal submission and humility.

5. Call a friend with a young child and tell them you are babysitting for them this coming weekend—just because you love them and wish to relieve some weight in their lives.

8

Questions and Answers

IS IT POSSIBLE FOR THOSE OUTSIDE OF THE GOSPEL FAMILY TO EXPERIENCE TRUE COMMUNITY?

This book is about community—doing life together in a way that makes sense and in a way that matters on the landscape of eternity. While the scope of this book is within the boundaries of Christian community, someone recently asked me if what I am talking about is possible for a person who is not a follower of Jesus. At first, I didn't offer an answer. Like other questions in which I don't immediately have a clear answer, it was helpful for me to sit with it and then to reframe it. So I asked it this way: Is it possible for those who do not know Jesus, who do not treasure Jesus-centered relationships and have no working reality of the pursuit of holiness, to actually experience the kind of community we're after?

The reason this question is of paramount importance is because if the answer is yes, then you might as well put this book down. If the answer to that question is yes, then the apostle Paul would be right in saying, ". . .we are to be the most pitied of all people" (1 Corinthians 15:19). If the what of our lives (Jesus' death, burial, resurrection and Spirit filling), doesn't really change the how of doing life with people, then why would any Christian submit his life, time, dreams, money, and attitudes to others over the long haul? That is, if the goal isn't to become more like Jesus, then real community is truly up for grabs.

Unfortunately, all relationships will fall short apart from the breath of God on them. True, honest, loving, faithful, and burden-bearing community can only ever be found when it is God-centered and Christ-exalting. And yet a desire for deep relationship is bred deeply into our DNA as humans, not just as Christians. The echo from our Creator still lingers, "It is not good for man to be alone" (Genesis 2:18). Or perhaps the eternity that was set in our hearts (Ecclesiastes 3:10)—that which was expressed by Solomon and has been experienced by all—was not only a need for God, but also a deep need for people.

People, all people, are image bearers of God. That means humans reflect the divine nature of God to other people. Or to put it another way—our image-bearing gives us our picture of where we belong in the universe. We are God's. We belong to him. We are meant for him. This truth resounds from the mouth of the twenty-four elders in heaven, "You are worthy to take the scroll and to open its seals, because you were slain, and with your blood you purchased for God persons from every tribe and language and people and nation" (Revelation 5:9).

People are made for God. Jesus did not shed His blood simply so that men and women would serve God. We are made to be known—known by people and by God. But not everyone knows God. Many have rejected Jesus and many more have yet to hear about the work of God on their behalf. That means those people will believe they are made for something other than relationship—money; fame; the American dream. But their lack of relationship with the Creator notwithstanding, they still long for deep community. Gospel redemption does not awaken a need for community, it simply gives it real meaning. Just because a neighbor doesn't have a relationship with Christ doesn't mean they don't want deep relationships with people. And rightly so, those outside the community of faith have been pursuing deep relationships for millennia.

Jason is a friend of mine who, at one time, was a follower of Jesus. He would not call himself that any longer. For many years he battled same sex attraction, and he finally gave up, left his wife, and subsequently left the church. Many in the church treated him badly. I was embarrassed and ashamed of those of us on the inside. Hours of conversation with Jason ensued and I assured him that he would be walking a very lonely road apart from his faith family. In the beginning that was a true statement. But over the course of three or four months, I saw less and less of Jason. One day I invited him to lunch and I asked him, "Where are you? Who are you doing life with now?" Jason went on to describe a community of people that he had met and found real affinity with. They shared the commonality of a broken past of same sex attraction, present frustrations with the church, and disillusionment with family. He told me that he finally felt like home. Jason found a kind of community.

Barry used to be a pastor. His church tanked and almost closed its doors. That was the last straw in his already fractured faith. Like a growing number of disillusioned pastors, he waved goodbye to organized and intentional gospel community and is now seeking "spiritual" relationships somewhere else, preferably as far away from the church as he can get. He's now a manager of a clothing store and spends his weekends on the lake. Barry has lots of friends. He is kind and funny and inviting. Because he used to be so involved in the city, he and his wife regularly have people in their home to share meals and good conversation. Barry too has found a form of community.

Mary and Stephen have never really been to church. Easter a few years ago was their first church experience. Both are professors and have always felt that Christianity was not intellectually engaging. They have rebuffed invitations and have been quite honest in saying they are not interested in doing life with Jesus people. Instead, during the fall they travel around the southeast, following their favorite football team. Their camper takes them to the next tailgating destination. And of course, tailgating isn't simply an activity, it's a form of religion. People gather, elements of communion (beer and hotdogs) are distributed, the exaltation of smash mouth football is celebrated, and the community of friends disperse, looking forward to the next assembly of the saints. Mary and Stephen have been tailgating with the same people for 25 years. And they are deeply committed to these people. They've cheered on new babies, attended graduations, and have mourned at their fair share of funerals. Mary and Stephen have a kind of community.

Sam just lost his wife to cancer. It was a long battle which no one could win. After the funeral he walked into a home that is now empty, but used to be a source of joy and lively activity. All of Sam's friendships have disappeared, primarily because he spent most moments in the last three years caring for his wife. Sam decided to join a survivor's support group. They eat together, share pictures of the ones they've lost, and even comfort each other in their grief. What started out as a Tuesday afternoon grief meeting has now blossomed into bowling nights and Parcheesi parties. Sam has found a community that has filled a gap.

Community is possible apart from Jesus. It is. Just not the kind of community that drives people to love God and lay down their lives for something greater than themselves. But a community that meets a real need nonetheless.

Jason shares his life with people who understand his past and accept him for who he is. Barry has found a group of people who seem to genuinely care for him but no longer ask anything of him. Mary and Stephen have discovered life around a shared activity. And Sam has tasted community because others shared his pain. But is that enough? Can shared experiences and common frailty carry us through to the end? I don't think so. And frankly, I believe it's the wrong question. Not, Is it enough? but Why not more? Why aren't people expecting more from their friendships, marriages, BFF's, and church small groups? Are our expectations of God's grace so low that we have settled for football, fellowships, and shared pain as the gold standard for gospel community? If God has promised us abundant life in the here and now, surely some of that is meant for our relationships!

King David sang in Psalm 42, "Deep calls out to deep . . ." Deep places of life, pain, birth, and death call out to the deep places of eternity. The voices of man cry out to God for more! Sinners and saints all have an innate need to go deep with other people. But those who are far from God don't know where deep is. They are image bearers but still don't having their bearings. And because of that reality, deep gets translated into authentic or real or non-judgmental or mysterious. And yet the deep that all men and women long for is only found anchored in the unending well of the mercy of Jesus Christ. Real community is only found in Christ, his people, and the mission of the kingdom of God.

HOW IS THE LANGUAGE OF PRAYER DEVELOPED IN COMMUNITY?

Praying is like swimming. We learn to do it by doing it. We'd love to jump in the water and splash around, but we're afraid the water might be too deep. We settle for simply reading about the water, studying the appropriate technique of the breaststroke and keenly watching others as they dive in.

Many never actually get wet. This is why prayer is meant to be learned in community. Lifeguards abound in this prayer pool. We are meant to pray together. Learning the language, the rhythm, and the Person behind prayer is the goal. This is not an academic pursuit. We are not parsing out the verbs in the Lord's Prayer. But we are teaching. This is not a school of appropriate prayers for appropriate times, but we will teach when to pray and when to listen.

A plentitude of books on prayer have not necessarily spurred on prayer. Dozens of books which reflect on the nature and modes of intercession are on my shelf, but those books are only artifacts as we dig deep together into the action of prayer. We are prayerless, not because we don't have the right tools, but because we don't have the right people around us, praying before us and with us.

Jesus himself was asked by his disciples, "Teach us to pray." He prefaced his teaching with a few guidelines and reminders: 1. Don't pray like religious people, who want to be seen. 2. Don't keep babbling on like a broken record, to be heard. 3. God already knows what you need.

These three guidelines give us the nudge to step off dry ground into the water. "And when you pray, do not be like the hypocrites, for they love to pray standing in the synagogues and on the street corners to be seen by others. Truly I tell you, they have received their reward in full. But when you pray, go into your room, close the door and pray to your Father, who is unseen. Then your Father, who sees what is done in secret, will reward you" (Matthew 6:5–6).

Prayer isn't about talking loudly or getting God's attention. We don't shout so that God can hear our prayers. He isn't the hard-of-hearing geriatric that we have been led to believe he is. He is active. Actively listening, in fact. We are heard because God has His ear toward us (1 John 5:14). We are heard because the veil between the most holy and the most unholy has been torn in two. God was not unavailable before the cross, but he was unapproachable. Nothing can enter his throne room without the fingerprint of righteousness. And so the cross is the way for grace to flood the earth. The blood of Jesus has now made God available and approachable. We can now enter into his gates with thanksgiving (Psalm 100:4) and come before his throne with boldness (Hebrews 4:16). We don't speak to God as strangers any longer, but as sons and daughters.

This is the theology of prayer. That is, we were far away from God. Cursed of God. Objects of wrath. Then Jesus drew near, became a curse for us and took on the wrath we deserved. We became the righteousness of God (2 Corinthians 5:21).

Prayer is first a practice of theology. Not that a person can't pray without any knowledge of this deep truth. Children and the unknowing pray to the Unknowable because there is an instinct, an eternity in our hearts (Ecclesiastes 3:11). But in community we can't be allowed to take this beautiful reality for granted. Redeemed hearts are naturally inclined to long for God's heart. But they don't really know what to pray, how to pray. So we teach them by praying it out loud, in community. We help push aside the fear of praying out loud by first praying out loud with them. What was in the darkness is now in the light. Praying is not scary, only unknown. We ask those we walk with to pray for us. Even though we could pray better prayers, more eloquent prayers, more informed prayers, we ask them to pray for us. We present our very real needs that they are unable to meet and we ask them to ask God on our behalf. Out loud. This is the way people learn to pray. There are no missteps in these first prayer sessions. We don't scold our toddler for not knowing the right things to say and how to ask appropriately. For a while we just settle for lots of grunts and whines and pointing. Learning to pray is much like that. Over time, however, words and ideas are adopted. The words become the language of prayer.

Ultimately, we pray theology. We pray, but we want to pray the deep things of God. This is how we teach who God is and what he has done. Of course, these prayers are born out of the scriptures and the riches of the written gospel narrative. But not unlike the first 15 centuries, the gospel and its language is first spoken, then read. We are first a verbal tradition.

Praying theology does not necessarily mean formality in prayer. I am deeply protestant and value off-the-cuff, "real prayers" from the heart. But if prayers are only emotionally driven and predicated only on our needs, they are not very real. Shallow at best, rote and superficial. Diving deep into the language of the cross, Jesus' blood, resurrection, new bodies and future glory, gives teeth to our prayers. We must teach this language as we pray. We're not really after our people sounding like theologians, but we do want them thinking and praying that way.

". . . for your Father knows what you need before you ask him" (Matthew 6:8). Prayer is developed in the most natural way too. We pray what we need. It couldn't be any less spiritual than that! What do you need? Let's pray for it! We must make it OK, even natural, to pray out of a deficit. But we also pray knowing he doesn't need us to pray. He is sovereign over all things. "The Lord is in the heavens, he does whatever he pleases" (Psalm 115:3). There is nothing that can derail God's plan or add to it. And yet, and this is the mystery of prayer, when we pray, heaven moves. Heaven doesn't jump to attention as if a fire alarm has gone off in fire station 12, making angels aware of an emergency in Cleveland. God already knows. And yet, prayer moves him. We pray, and something happens. Any theologian who says they understand it is lying.

This kind of prayer culminates in a statement—Your will be done. Your will be done is the kindergarten and the graduate school of prayer. Babies in the faith and Desert Fathers learn this in every new season of life. And because community is meant to be lived over the long arc of years, we teach it in community. This is not the prayer of a fatalist, however. *Whatever is going to happen is going to happen, so why pray?* No! This is the prayer of maturity. He knows what we need and that is why we pray Your will be done. He may know we need humility and so he wills suffering—Your will be done. If he knows that we need to learn to be under authority and he wills that we are put in an unjust workplace—Your will be done. He knows when we seek unhealthy satisfaction in our romances, and he may will that we are alone so that we might find our joy in him—Your will be done. He already knows of the financial need, but he wills that you suffer loss—Your will be done. Or a great financial windfall—your will be done. In every circumstance, in every loss and gain—Your will be done.

This must be the river that all prayers flow down. On occasion we teach it by teaching it—chapter and verse. But mostly, we teach it by the way we pray, by the way we live. Your will be done in the best times of life and in the worst. "Naked I came into this world, naked I will depart. The Lord gives and the Lord takes away. May the name of the Lord be praised" (Job 1:21). Circumstances often determine what we pray, but never how we pray. Your will be done.

The power of prayer is rooted in the power and sufficiency of God to do what he says he will do. But it is also in knowing how powerless and insufficient we are. Help your community put on display their suffering and pain in prayer. Help them see that they don't have to decorate their loss with flowery language when a cry of pain will do. Teach your community by praying, not just talking about prayer, that God will be welcome in every area of life.

WHAT ABOUT PASTORS?

If doctors make the worst patients, pastors make the worst community members. We teach community, point to it in the narrative of scripture and life; we plead to those we serve to give themselves to it. But pastors are incessantly lonely, isolated, and far from community. I often wonder, How can we believe in something so profoundly and not live it out?

When we were sharing this idea with those in our little community, someone quipped, Of course! Is there a time pastors can take off the pastor hat and just be normal people? I thought, that's true. Can pastors lead and shepherd and at the same time become supremely vulnerable with those same people? The answer is yes, but not easily. Several problems face every pastor hoping to be part of life-giving, long-term community.

First, the tenure of local church pastors is getting shorter. Decades ago it would not have been unusual for a pastor to stay with a people for 30 years. They would be fresh out of bible-college with a tiny U-Haul trailing an eager young couple who were idealistic not just about people, but also about the church. They would have every intention of driving their roots down deep into this city, cultivating a church to become a family in which to raise children, watch a city change, and grow old with a few. Church used to be less of an assignment and more a place to drop anchor for life. Now however, the average stay of an American pastor is three years.[1] Just long enough for a pastor to cast a compelling vision, preach his best sermons, and begin to cultivate relationships that matter before "a calling" to another church beckons. This calling is sometimes less about God and more about something else—often an unhealthy ambition to preach to larger crowds or boast a more fruitful budget. And often, the culprit is an unwillingness to face difficult people and have hard gospel conversations that bring about unity and reconciliation. Some pastors are consummate hope-stealers. Rug-pullers. Preaching of a potential future, a promised land, with no intention of leading the people there themselves.

Pastors, and I hate to admit this, are often the most insecure people on the planet. We long for the praise of men from afar but fear the sting of correction up close. Power is not something we necessarily cling to, but when others laud it over us it makes our eyes prone to wander to greener grass. Pastors want to go deep, build upon the living stones of Jesus' church, and have the community they so eloquently speak about, but it's just too hard to stay. We are cowards.

Secondly, pastors don't often have a deep, cultivated soul that is prepared for what community demands. This is not an indictment. Just an

---

1. Thom Rainer, "The Dangerous Third Year of Pastoral Tenure," Last Modified June 18, 2014, Last Accessed August 2, 2018, http://thomrainer.com/2014/06/dangerous-third-year-pastoral-tenure/

observation. Pastors can be shallow. Not all pastors. In fact, I know dozens of pastors who have a deep, robust relationship with Jesus in which they are making war viciously against their sin, preaching with tears for the repentance of their people, and have zero desire to become a celebrity in the church world. They aren't complaining about the small pay and long hours. They count it an honor to pour out their lives for the sake of Jesus' bride. Their ministry is only an outlet for the passion of their lives. But as many pastors as I know who are like that, there are as many who are coasting, clinging to a paycheck, and just don't like people. I'm not sure what happened. At one time, these pastors wanted to make a difference with the upside down kingdom. But then the rose colored glasses of seminary were replaced with the disdain of church politics and geriatric entitlement. The camaraderie of friends who would one day win a city has been replaced with counting down the days till retirement.

Let me say, before you label me a pastoral troublemaker, I love pastors. I am one. I believe the vocation of pastor is the greatest privilege and honor for all men or women. As Charles Spurgeon is famous for saying, "Why stoop to become a king, when I can be a pastor?" But for all the time we are being prepared to parse a Greek word or champion the cause of Reformation Solas, we are terribly unequipped for the breakneck speed and demands of shepherding a people. Pastors begin full of life and grace and vision, but life and grace and vision get sucked out of them by the very ministry they pledged their life to. This is why pastoring requires someone to be a marine, a counselor, a CEO, an ambassador, and a priest. What is asked of us is just short of impossible. And because the immanent possibility of failure looms, so many pastors settle in their hearts to do the least that is required in ministry. It isn't success, but it's not failure either. The problem is that vulnerable, sin-killing, and long-term community is not typically in the minimum job description of the pastor. So he does the least to get by, and his penance is isolation.

Third, churches aren't built for this paradigm of deep community. Let's face it, churches are built for volume. Like the modern big box store, churches are designed to drive the masses through the doors, meet as many needs as possible in one hour, and then herd them out to their cars to make way for the rest of the sheep. I have no disdain for the church. She is a mess, but she is still the bride of Christ. I love the church. I love that billions around the world gather every weekend to sit in rows, under the authority of the bible, to have the unfiltered Word of God spoken over them, celebrate the resurrection of Jesus through communion, and then leave on mission. Instead of joining the ranks of so many who have decided to abandon the church for something more organic or natural or less authoritarian or less bossy or whatever the current accusation, I encourage men and women to stay and appreciate what God is doing around them. In fact, I've never met a person who has left the corporate church and found themselves more white-hot for Jesus. I've never met a person who has left the corporate church and found the community they're made for. The larger church and the smaller church community go hand-in-hand. We are meant for both.

This brings us back to pastors. Pastors lead churches that don't often have a paradigm for deep community. The metric for church success does not typically include this kind of personal or corporate rhythm. Perhaps there are classes and recovery programs and even workshops to help exhausted parents, but these aren't what we're talking about when we reference deep community. Starting points, but not the destination. This is rarely the pastor's fault. Sometimes a pastor steps into a church which would take decades to steer toward this ideal. And often he or she will. But more often, it will feel like an impossibility and it won't even be attempted. This kind of church structure makes it problematic for a pastor to cultivate this ethos, let alone develop it in his own life.

So what are pastors to do? Where do we go? If our vocation, hearts, and structure seem to be warring against us, how do we overcome? As I finish answering this question, let me speak directly to pastors.

First, seek relational depth with those you lead. If there are a few people that are walking alongside you, partnering with you in the work of ministry, then these people may understand your unique position. You share common language, mission, compassion, and calling and are all in the pressure cooker of ministry together. Create time outside of the church world to eat together, share life together, raise kids together. No need to rehash the day's events or talk about the next church event. Put away the calendar and the complaining and try to enjoy each other. God put your families together so that you can go the distance in life, not necessarily just in ministry.

Second, find other local pastors outside of your church. These men and women are not your competition or rival or enemy. We know that to be true, but we don't often behave that way. We see them in the marketplace and give them the appropriate spiritual greeting, but as they walk away, we give them a suspicious sideways glance. In the more honest moments of our day we suspect they are just as lonely and uncertain as we are.

Third, learn to go deep with those outside of your church. Our city hosts an organization that connects pastors to one another. That's all they do. It is facilitated by a retired pastor who led a local church for thirty years. He understands how jacked-up church leaders can be. So he gives all his time to make sure pastors are in community. Last year he connected me with two other local pastors. I was suspicious of Shaun and Ben. I wasn't sure I would really get along with these guys. Both are gifted and charismatic leaders. I am highly insecure. I agreed to a lunch with these guys, that was it. A probation period at best. What I found, however, was that these guys were just like me. In fact, there was such an ease in our initial meeting that it gave me the willies. It turns out there is a shorthand language that all pastors know. We all have these intense feelings and pressures that only another pastor would understand. I didn't have to explain to them about a problem person or a difficult leadership moment—they had them too! I didn't have to explain in detail the supreme challenge of expectations and family and ambition. They already felt those. After we discovered what a gift this community was to ourselves and each other, we committed to meet together every month. We eat together, read a book together, and pray together. It is one of the most important things I schedule. In fact, now our wives have gotten into the mix.

HOW DO YOU START OVER?

Not all community experiments work. Sometimes they blow up. No amount of good conversation, late night laughs, and solid chemistry can move a community group to the place of gospel deeps. As you have read, Amy and I have our fair share of scars and wounds and hurt feelings because of failed community experiments. Joe and Patty are just one true-life example of how hard this beautiful promise can be. It was good; then it wasn't; and now it is good again, but different.

I'm always surprised when I discover certain people I know have divorced. They were people that had everything going for them and yet, for whatever reason, the marriage imploded. Everyone scratches their heads. Then there are couples that have nothing in common, lose a child, the company goes belly-up and somehow, they make it work. They thrive even. Still, everyone scratches their heads.

My hope for you is that people move into the foyer of your life, then into the dining room, and eventually into the beautiful places of intimacy that last decades. My prayer for you is that you look around at those God has brought around you and you pinch yourself. I'm hoping. Praying.

Though sometimes community takes more than is available. More work, more chemistry, more grace, more energy, more wisdom. Unfortunately, the more we need often eludes us until it's too late. Sometimes starting over is inevitable. Sometimes people move, change communities, get divorced, take correction poorly, and leave. Sometimes a good season is followed by a really bad season and we realize everyone is gone. So we have to start over. When this happens, I remind myself of three things:

This community isn't about me. This is about God. Like marriage, gospel community puts on display the glory and mercy of Jesus. Walking in relationship with others challenges our selfishness and our entitlement that seeks to always make life about us. When life and relationships don't seem to work out the way I intend, I remind myself that convenience is not something I want to depend on or lean into. Starting over means holding on to the grace of God even harder. It means remembering how good God has been to me over the decades and that his goodness has not yet come to an end. Starting over is one more opportunity to set God on the throne of my life and remind him (not that he needs reminding) that he is in charge of all things, including my relationships. He is able to bring who he wants into my life and, in his wisdom, he is able to remove them. Starting over is an opportunity for me to humble myself. Starting over is a chance for me to kill whatever pride might be lingering in my heart. Opening up my home (again) is a chance for God to do something I couldn't have even imagined was possible . . . one more time.

When I start over, I also need to remind myself that this is about others. God wants to use me, for the sake of others. His desire is that my gifts (and yours), whether they be teaching or mercy or administration, be used in community, for the good of others. I am not allowed to cry foul when I do not get my way or when people don't caress my ego. It is not the job of the people who surround me to meet every deep need I have. That is not their job. That is the role of Jesus. When you sit in a living room once again with a new set of people, remind yourself of the supreme privilege you have to serve them and invest in them over the long arc of time. Whether it be three months or thirty years, love them well. Whether they ever realize your investment or intention, it doesn't matter, because this is not about you, it is about them. It is about their good, their heart being spurred on to greater Christlikeness.

Lastly, I remind myself of this surprising truth: this is about me and you. I know I just said it wasn't about you, but it's sort of about you. Maybe I should have said this isn't primarily about you. But God loves you. He is for you and for your ultimate sanctification and satisfaction. He wants to fill your heart with good things and for you to be caught up in the wonder of his grace. He intends that you would finish your race. His prayer for you is that you would be in unity with others and the local church. He is primarily concerned about your life being whole and holy and orbiting around the grace of Jesus. Life and community is mostly about God's glory, but you're in the picture as well. His design is to put lonely people in families; heal the broken hearted; bind up the wounded; fill them with peace; and set them on mission. You are not the treasure of the universe, but you are treasured by God. And he loves you so much that he desires to see you (and me) walk deeply in grace, bound up in the unity of the church, and in ferocious pursuit of God's best, with others. When starting over in community, take courage that God has a beautiful plan that will unfold in his perfect timing.

HOW MUCH IS THIS PROCESS OF CULTIVATING COMMUNITY JUST MYSTERY?

The answer to this question is two-fold. On one hand, this thing we're in search of is deeply tactile and physical. Jesus came into the world—in flesh, not in Spirit. He didn't phone in the mission of God. It took every ounce of who he was, in person, to accomplish the love of the Father for us. In other words, Jesus was human and his humanity was deeply connected to other humans. It had to be. He rubbed shoulders with Peter and John. He reached down and kissed his mother. He ate long, enjoyable meals with friends. He mourned the loss of a brother and the rebellion of a city. He sweated and ached and even had bad breath. Jesus was fully flesh. Without sin, but fully human. It was only because he was wholly human and touchable that he was also able to be beaten and tortured and crucified on our account.

Community, at least in the mechanics of it, is not mysterious. Natural even.

Exhausting too. Exhausting is an apt description that reminds us that our physical selves must be present in this thing we do. We give and take. Give and take. In fragile, underdeveloped community it will feel like we are giving much more than we are taking. Again, this is the natural, in person, fully-present result of community.

At the same time, community feels enigmatic and hard to pin down—at least when something good is happening. Mysterious is an appropriate adjective for those moments in community that are so good in spite of our bumblings. Like seeing a rainbow or sunset—we see it and savor it with wonder, knowing we had nothing to do with it. And even though there are scientific explanations of light refraction and scattering molecules changing the direction of rays of sunlight, we still look upon them with our mouth half agape. We actually prefer the mystery of what is before us. Explaining it would, in fact, ruin it. We prefer to hold onto God's little mercies at the end of a hard week. We drive home fuming over a failed meeting and look up at the blues and pinks and yellows streaking together to form a canvas of splendor, reminding us that beauty serves no other purpose but to delight. That little clandestine mercy of our prodigal God should cause us to wonder about his wastefulness, his generosity, his showering of beauty on the likes of us. Why would he give us such a gift that we haven't cultivated on our own? Grace. Mercy. His kindness. Looking around a table with friends, knowing I am reaping where I have not sown (John 4:38), I have the same feeling.

I've always loved how C.S. Lewis imagines the creation of the world in *The Magician's Nephew*. God creates with a song. Is there anything more unpredictable than a melody coming out of the mouth of God? This song setting atoms and matter ablaze. Trees and fruit coming out of the dust. Creatures breathing in their first. Aslan's song makes things that were not already:

> "The eastern sky changed from white to pink and from pink to gold. The Voice rose and rose, till all the air was shaking with it. And just as it swelled to the mightiest and most glorious sound it had yet produced, the sun arose. Digory had never seen such a sun. The sun above the ruins of Charn had looked older than ours: this looked younger. You could imagine that it laughed for joy as it came up. And as its beams shot across the land the travellers could see for the first time what sort of place they were in. It was a valley through which a broad, swift river wound its way, flowing eastward towards the sun. Southward there were mountains, northward there were lower hills. But it was a valley of mere earth, rock and water; there was not a tree, not a bush, not a blade of grass to be seen. The earth was of many colours: they were fresh, hot and vivid. They made you feel excited; until you saw the Singer himself, and then you forgot everything else."[2]

---

2. C.S. Lewis, The Chronicles of Narnia, (New York, NY: Harper Collins, 2001), 62

We take for granted this kind of supernatural work; likely because we weren't present at the beginning and we don't think of ourselves as creators. It's an impossibility to feel the weight of what happened when God spoke the universe and our world into being. Words like "big bang" are often the only concepts the world can muster to aptly describe something so otherly. But God's people, we are not so far removed from what creation is. Mostly because we are still in it and woven into its fabric. We have a deep, intrinsic connection to the stuff of this world.

God is still in the creation business—singing, seeing, celebrating new things right now. We have a generous Creator and he stirs up the hearts of billions of little creators (you and me). Could it be that he takes special pride in us, his little image bearers, as we imitate him, seeking to create? We are literally creative types. All of us. Many of us would not wear that label, of course. We have been trained, boxed in to our place in the world. Clean lines, definable roles, and no surprises. That is what is expected from us. We find our place and step into an identity that marks us for 70 years.

You might be called accountant. Or manager. Factory worker or poet. Plumber or house painter. Creative or non-creative are the only two categories this world offers. Creative or non-creative. Is it possible, though, that we're all creatives? This prospect makes our world nervous. Department managers and wardens of cubicle prisons get afraid when they hear these whispers. They become afraid of wild things because of what might happen if the prisoner realizes the gates have been left open. We begin to come alive to "the more" of abundant living that is realized in community. Fully alive men and women disrupt the death march of the forty year, gold watch goal. It's almost like a waking dream in which old power structures that have been keeping us trapped in black and white have been torn down and HD color is available to anyone who wants it.

The confession that we are all creatives is a confession in which the natural and supernatural come together. Heaven and earth collide when we open up the door to our home. A deep mystery in some way begins to make sense.

Bibliography

Froude, James Anthony. The History of England: From the Fall of Wolsey to the Defeat of the Spanish Armada, (London, Longmans, Green & Co, 1893)

Junger, Sabastian. Tribe: On Homecoming and Belonging, (New York, Hatchett Book Group, 2016)

Lewis, C.S. The Chronicles of Narnia, (New York, Harper Collins, 2001)

McGregor, Jena, "The Average Workweek is Now 47 Hours," Washington Post, September 2, 2014. https://www.washingtonpost.com/news/on-leadership/wp/2014/09/02/the-average-work-week-is-now-47-hours (Accessed September 2018)

Nachfolger, Hermann Boehlaus, "The Last Written Words of Luther," 1909, http://www.iclnet.org/pub/resources/text/wittenberg/luther/beggars.txt (Accessed June 4, 2018)

Parr, Ben, "Social Networking Accounts for 1 of Every 6 Minutes Spent Online," Mashable, June 15, 2011, https://mashable.com/2011/06/15/social-networking-accounts-for-1-of-every-6-minutes-spent-online-stats/#3iACAK9uy5qz (Accessed June 2, 2018).

Piper, John. A Peculiar Glory, (Wheaton, Crossway, 2016)

Rainer, Thom, "The Dangerous Third Year of Pastoral Tenure,," ThomRainer, June 18, 2014, https://thomrainer.com/2014/06/dangerous-third-year-pastoral-tenure/, (Accessed August 2, 2018)

www.ingramcontent.com/pod-product-compliance
Lightning Source LLC
Chambersburg PA
CBHW072149160426
43197CB00012B/2307